Developing a Successful
TUTORING PROGRAM

TITLES IN THE TUTORING SERIES

by Patricia S. Koskinen and Robert M. Wilson

Developing a Successful Tutoring Program (for teachers and school administrators)

Tutoring: A Guide for Success (for adult tutors)

A Guide for Student Tutors

Developing a Successful
TUTORING PROGRAM

Patricia S. Koskinen and Robert M. Wilson
Reading Center, College of Education
University of Maryland at College Park

Teachers College, Columbia University, New York and London 1982

Published by Teachers College Press, 1234 Amsterdam Avenue,
New York, N.Y. 10027

Library of Congress Cataloging in Publication Data

Koskinen, Patricia S., 1942–
  Developing a successful tutoring program.

  (Tutoring series)
  Bibliography: p.
  Includes index.
  1. Tutors and tutoring.   I.   Wilson, Robert Mills.
II.   Title.   III.   Series: Koskinen, Patricia, 1942–
Tutoring series.
LC41.K67   371.3'94   81-18335
                                AACR2

ISBN 0-8077-2673-7

Manufactured in the United States of America

87   86   85   84   83   82   1   2   3   4   5   6

Contents

Preface

The purpose of this book is to provide guidelines and ideas for those desiring to initiate a tutoring program in their schools. The tutoring movement has become an important aspect of schooling. Once we realized the importance of the one-to-one relationship which tutoring can offer, we searched for ways to implement tutoring programs. This book is the result of our years of experience with various types of programs.

Tutoring programs differ in many ways depending on the needs of participating students. As you use this book, you will want to adapt our suggestions to the unique needs of your program. You will find, however, that this book is organized so that many of the ideas can easily be applied without adjustment.

Two books have been prepared as companions to this volume. *Tutoring: A Guide for Success* is a guide for adult tutors. Because of the many ideas and guidelines for tutoring, adult tutors in the school's program will benefit from having their own copies. *A Guide for Student Tutors* is for students who work as tutors. This book is designed to allow each student tutor to write in his or her copy and readily refer to the specific tips for tutoring. These two books will be valuable references to tutors as they work with their students.

A tutoring program takes time and effort to develop but will provide exciting benefits for everyone involved: administrators, tutors, and students. If you add generous amounts of enthusiasm, caring, and organization to the ideas in this book, your program will be off to a successful beginning.

College Park, Md., 1982   P.S.K.
                                                                  R.M.W.

Acknowledgments

The pleasure of writing these books in the tutoring series was enhanced by the many people who contributed their ideas, suggestions, and enthusiastic support. Special appreciation is extended to the many coordinators of tutoring programs and tutors and their students whose excitement about their work stimulated us to write this book.

We are particularly grateful to John Koskinen who has been a skillful editor as well as a continuous source of encouragement. Marti King's reactions to the initial draft of our first manuscript were also especially helpful. We are indebted to Darryl Henry and Sandra Weiswasser for the warm, loving pictures they took of tutors and their students.

Other friends have also given generously of their time and expertise. Susan Coles and Sharon Villa provided not only expert typing but continuous patience and good cheer. Thomas Higgs contributed a number of creative illustrations for the text. Finally we appreciate the help of Lois Patton, Louise Craft, and Abby Levine, our editors, who have given us excellent advice and guided the final development of these books.

Developing a Successful
Tutoring Program

1 Introduction

ORGANIZER

This chapter contains a rationale for establishing a tutoring program and an overview of the elements involved in such a program.

If you are interested in:

- the rationale, see page 2.
- an overview of the facets of a program, see page 3.

If you have your own rationale and do not need to read an overview, then go directly to chapter 2, "The Tutoring Program Coordinator."

RATIONALE

Students in various circumstances need more individual attention than most teachers can offer. Some students tend to misunderstand assignments, allow their attention to wander, disrupt the work of others, and miss opportunities to learn. One solution to the need for individual attention is to provide such students with tutors. When students know that someone cares and that individual attention is being provided, their academic performance often improves.

Other students need more individual attention because of excessive illness and absence from school. While it is very difficult for teachers to take the time needed to help these students catch up, it is a relatively easy task for a tutor who has only that objective in mind.

Still other students need individual attention because for some reason they have missed the mastery of a subskill and are, as a result, not able to profit from instruction. Teachers who teach diagnostically are usually aware of such problems but often lack the time to give makeup instruction. A tutor can provide this time. As the student regains confidence, normal instruction becomes effective.

Students receiving tutoring help are not the only ones who profit. Classmates benefit as an otherwise distracted student begins to focus on learning. Teachers gain as the student becomes a successful learner. Parents see their child happy and successful instead of sad and frustrated. The total school population generally benefits from seeing a tutoring program as a helping program in which learning is important.

In some cases the person who profits most from the tutoring experience is the tutor. Tutors learn to be responsible for someone else's needs and must master the skills that they are to impart. As they develop a caring relationship for another person, tutors learn that such a relationship is a very positive one.

Because tutoring programs are inexpensive to operate, they

greatly increase the teaching potential of the staff at minimal cost. Some programs have no expense whatever, yet they bring resources to a school that are otherwise not available.

In light of the benefits tutoring programs provide for all involved, their substantial growth in recent years is not surprising. What is surprising is that every school does not generate this additional resource for its students.

OVERVIEW OF TUTORING PROGRAMS

Effective tutoring programs may differ in a variety of ways. An overview of some of the differences is provided so that anyone initiating a program can be aware of the many possibilities.

Purposes.   General purposes for tutoring usually fall into two major categories: the development of skills and the enhancement of self-concept. A tutoring program may focus on the development of academic skills such as reading or mathematics, physical skills such as tumbling, or creative skills in the areas of drama or music. In addition to skill development, an overall goal of most tutoring programs is to help students feel good about themselves and about learning in general.

Other goals might be established for specific programs. These include:

1.   providing an experience otherwise not available to the students, such as instruction in English for a student who speaks only a foreign language.
2.   providing enrichment activities. For example, a photographer might give lessons on good picture-taking, or a person who has just returned from Mexico might enliven a unit of study on that country.
3.   assisting the teacher in the classroom. For example, a teacher might be tape-recording a student reading a story. A tutor might supervise the recording, permitting the teacher to attend to other instructional activities.

Content.   There is no limitation to the content areas that can be included in a tutoring program. Excellent programs have been developed in reading, mathematics, science, health, art, music, industrial arts, and athletics.

Types of Tutors.   The most available source of tutors is in the school itself, with older children helping younger ones. Students from nearby schools have been used effectively, and college students tend to be willing tutors. Another large resource is parents or other adults from the community, especially retired citizens, who have much to offer.

Types of Students.   From preschool children to adults, tutoring needs can be found. Students range from mentally or physically disabled persons to the gifted and talented. Those confined to prisons and detention centers are yet another target population. Migrant workers' children have special needs, as do children whose native language is not the language used for instruction.

Tutoring Schedules.   Time lengths vary from fifteen minutes to several hours. Time can be scheduled during school as well as before and after. Sessions can be scheduled daily or once a week, and occasionally a single tutoring session for a specific purpose is sufficient.

Administration.   All tutoring programs need someone to administer training and to schedule, coordinate, and evaluate activities. Tutoring coordinators have come from many backgrounds, both in the school and in the community.

Training Procedures.   All tutoring programs should provide training, which will vary considerably with the purposes of the program. The time needed for training may be very short or quite extended. Some sessions may take only one half hour, while others may require daily meetings for a week or two.

Training can be conducted by teachers, former tutors, outside consultants, school specialists, or administrators, depending upon the nature of the program desired.

Each of these elements of a tutoring program is discussed in detail in the following chapters.

2 The Tutoring Program Coordinator

ORGANIZER

This chapter focuses on the role and selection of the tutoring program coordinator.

If you are interested in:

- the responsibilities of the coordinator, see page 6.
- guidelines for selecting a coordinator, see page 7.

SINCE tutoring programs involve many persons—students being tutored, tutors, teachers, and other school personnel—an effective coordinator is essential. The efficiency of the participants will depend largely upon the skills of the person designated as coordinator.

RESPONSIBILITIES OF THE COORDINATOR

Initially the role of coordinator is determined by the type of tutoring program in the school and the extent of involvement by other school personnel. In some programs the coordinator may only be a manager and delegate most of the responsibility, while in others he or she may perform the major tasks. Regardless of who will do these jobs, there is a need for one person to oversee the many activities of a tutoring program. The following are a few of the major responsibilities of the coordinator:

Recruiting and Selecting Tutors. While the coordinator cannot assume total responsibility for this activity, he or she may be closely involved so that all the prescribed qualifications of tutors are met.

Training, Supervising, and Supporting Tutors. While some coordinators personally train the tutors, this function can easily be assumed by interested and knowledgeable teachers. The coordinator does, however, need to see that continued support and supervision are provided after initial training. The training should include both subject matter orientation and guidelines for dealing with different types of student behavior.

Acting as a Liaison Between School Personnel and Tutors. Whenever a number of people assume new roles in a school, there are continual orientation needs. Tutors need to learn about school routines, and school personnel may desire assistance in adapting

6

to the presence and interests of tutors. The coordinator can help facilitate communication between tutors and school personnel by being available to hear and observe their needs.

Selecting Students to Be Tutored. While the teacher normally selects students for tutoring, the coordinator may become involved by discussing the types of tutoring available and matching students with tutors. If the coordinator is a teacher or specialist in the school, then he or she might help select students for tutoring.

Handling Administrative Details. Attention to the details of a program can make the difference between a smooth, efficient operation and a poorly managed program that people feel wastes their time. Establishing tutoring schedules that suit tutor and teacher needs, notifying those involved when absences are to occur, and checking on supplies are only a few of the small but vital jobs that need careful attention.

SELECTING A COORDINATOR

Coordination of a tutoring program involves public relations and administrative skills. When a coordinator for a schoolwide tutoring program is selected, the following questions should be considered:

1. Is the person enthusiastic about the program?
2. Does the person demonstrate good communication skills?
3. Has the person experience with tutoring programs?
4. Has the person experience in managing the work of others?
5. Will the person be accepted by the school staff?

Since excellent coordinators have come from many different educational backgrounds, the qualifications of candidates are more important than their titles or positions. Retired teachers, parents, principals, experienced tutors, reading specialists, and classroom teachers have all successfully coordinated tutoring programs. All resources of the school community should be considered.

Within the school staff, specialists such as the librarian, counselor, or reading teacher may be interested in coordinating a tutoring program. Because their schedules are somewhat flexible, it is easier for them to fit the role of coordination into their daily routines. Classroom teachers have also coordinated tutoring programs but found that they needed to delegate some responsibilities so their classes would not be continually interrupted.

While many schools look first to their staff for coordination, many good coordinators have come from the community. Parents or community members who have tutored or taught previously may be ideally suited for the job. Just as we look for tutors from a variety of places, we should be able to draw from these same sources to find a coordinator.

3 Getting Started

ORGANIZER

This chapter contains suggestions for gaining principal and teacher support and an explanation of initial decisions that need to be made about the structure of the tutoring program.

If you are interested in:

- gaining principal support, see page 10.
- suggestions for finding interested teachers, see page 11.
- initial decisions for teachers, see page 13.

THE interest and enthusiasm of a school's principal and teachers are crucial to the success of a tutoring program. Many school programs do not reach maximum potential because the staff does not understand, value, or desire them. Careful planning will assure that the principal and teachers have an opportunity to become fully acquainted with the tutoring programs.

GAINING PRINCIPAL SUPPORT

As instructional leaders, school principals are in the position to make or break a tutoring program. It is essential to have their enthusiastic support. Usually they respond positively to such programs, but not always. Busy schedules, other priorities, unfavorable past experiences, and lack of information are just a few reasons why principals might not support a tutoring program.

The first step in beginning any tutoring program, therefore, is to meet with the principal and explain clearly how the program is to be run, the benefits to be derived from it, and the resources necessary. This presentation must be carefully prepared and well-organized if any principal is to gain confidence that a successful program is possible.

> One teacher who wanted tutors to help some of her students increase their vocabularies made a tentative plan for working with these tutors before she talked to the principal. She had already found a few parents who were interested in tutoring and thought she might find more through the neighborhood community center. She also outlined the times and places for tutoring and the type of tutor-training needed. By working out some of the details in advance, she was able to answer the principal's questions and find what questions she needed to ask to get the program started.

When the principal shows enthusiasm for the tutoring program, the coordinator needs to take several steps to assure continued support:

1. ask the principal to encourage teachers, tutors, and children to participate in the program
2. inform the principal of all meetings and activities related to the program
3. obtain commitments for space, materials, and funding
4. keep the principal informed of changes in plans

When the principal is less than enthusiastic, the program coordinator will want to take steps 2, 3, and 4. The coordinator must also assure the principal that the tutoring program will not make great demands on his or her time and energy needed for other priorities. It may be desirable to arrange for reluctant principals to observe a program in action. When they see a successful program and the benefits that accrue from it, they often become quite enthusiastic.

FINDING INTERESTED TEACHERS

Supportive teachers play a major role in helping tutors and students enjoy the program. Tutors do their best when working where their time and efforts are valued. Students are also most likely to be enthusiastic if their teachers are interested in their activities and easily schedule time for tutoring. A core of two or three enthusiastic teachers is enough to merit the initiation of a tutoring program and is preferable to a larger group that is only mildly interested.

Interested teachers have been identified in a number of ways. The following two approaches have been particularly effective:

1. In some schools, the principal and resource teachers already know teachers who want to participate in tutoring programs and only need some help in organization and tutor-training. Also, they may know teachers who have not mentioned a tutoring program but have expressed the need for specific help for certain students. With sufficient background information, these teachers might be delighted to have their students participate in a tutoring program.

2. Meeting with groups of teachers to present an overview of tutoring programs is a way of generating interest and enthusiasm. A fifteen-minute presentation at a faculty or team meeting about the benefits and organization of tutoring programs encourages teachers to think about how they might want to design their own programs.

> A resource teacher who wanted a tutoring program in his school began a presentation to the faculty by describing a program he had recently visited. In this program high school students were helping upper elementary students with addition and subtraction facts by playing math games. He described the benefits of individualized attention and the students' increased interest and skill in math. After discussing a specific program, he went on to talk generally about the many ways a tutoring program can be organized and the importance of meeting the needs of an individual school. He included examples of the different types of skills, training, and tutors that could be involved in a program. He gave just enough information to interest teachers and enable them to plan a program around their own needs.

If the teachers are given a short participation form to fill out after the meeting (see figure 1), the organizers of the program will know immediately who is interested in participating.

FIGURE 1   Tutoring Participation Form

Name _____   Grade/Level _____

I would like some of my students to participate in a tutoring program.

       YES_____   NO_____

Questions and/or comments

_____

_____

_____

_____

As tutoring gets under way and other teachers see the interested students and the quality of the tutoring activities, they usually begin requesting participation for their students.

MAKING INITIAL DECISIONS

Because teachers are responsible for the educational programs of their students, they need to be involved in decisions about the structure of the tutoring program. Organizers of tutoring programs need to know teachers' views concerning:

- the content of tutoring
- the frequency and length of tutoring sessions
- the length of the tutoring period
- the number of students to be tutored
- the extent of personal involvement in the program

The following section includes a variety of choices related to the structure of the tutoring program. Teachers who will be participating need to discuss these choices and make some group decisions. Giving teachers a questionnaire, such as the one shown in figure 2, helps focus attention on the important decisions in each area and also gives the program initiators useful written information for future planning.

Content of Tutoring.   Students with a wide range of ability have been tutored in almost all subject areas. Experience in developing tutoring programs has shown, however, that it is easier to make administrative arrangements and provide adequate initial and continuous training when only a few skill areas are at first selected. If teachers decide that their students need help in reading, they may begin by selecting students who need to be stimulated to read or who need to increase their sight vocabulary. Tutors would then be trained in ways to foster the enjoyment of books and in techniques to reinforce sight vocabulary. If the area of mathematics is selected, teachers may focus on one small area and decide to train tutors to first work on reinforcement ideas for addition, subtraction, or multiplication facts. (See

FIGURE 2 Teacher Questionnaire

Name_____   Grade/Level_____

1. I would like my students tutored in _____.

 reading   math   _____
                                                        other

 Specific skill area(s) _____

 _____

2. I would like my students tutored _____ per week.

 once   twice   three times   _____
                                                              other

3. I would like each tutoring session to be _____ minutes long.

 20   30   45   _____
                                        other

4. The tutoring period should be approximately _____ month(s) long.

5. I would like to have approximately _____ students participate in tutoring.

6. In addition to giving the tutors and students support, I would like to be further involved in the development of the tutoring program.
 YES_____   NO_____

 I would like to help:

 _____ recruit tutors   _____ train tutors   _____ other
 _____ screen tutors   _____ schedule tutoring   _____

Appendix F for a beginning list of activities that tutors have successfully used with students.)

Frequency and Length of Tutoring Sessions. The amount of time students are engaged in activities outside of class is of utmost concern to teachers. Tutoring sessions must be frequent enough to provide continuity for the student, yet the classroom program must remain relatively undisturbed. If tutoring is scheduled only once a week, the student may frequently miss this session due to schedule changes, special trips, and absence. Thus a schedule that provides sessions at least two times a week is desirable.

The length of a session should vary in relation to the purposes and ages of the students. A review of literature on tutoring (Koskinen, 1975) suggests that twenty to thirty minutes is appropriate for elementary age students, while high school students can easily work for longer periods (forty-five minutes to an hour). Generally a minimum of fifteen minutes is needed for getting settled, completing an activity, and planning for the future. Ten minutes should be allowed for the student to travel to and from the place of tutoring.

Length of a Tutoring Program. The amount of time students spend with a tutor may vary from a few sessions to many months. This period should be determined by the teacher's assessment of need together with student and tutor interest. For example, a tutor might help a group of students prepare food by following a recipe. Such an activity might involve the tutor for one session only. On the other hand, a tutor might work with a student to improve reading comprehension skills. This project would involve sessions lasting several months. When beginning a tutoring program, it is helpful to have a projected termination date and a planned evaluation time. With a clearly defined conclusion, tutors, teachers, and students can see their commitment within boundaries and may be more eager to participate.

A program lasting for six to eight weeks provides a sufficient amount of time for a relationship to develop between tutor and student and a range of skills to be reinforced. If the tutoring then stops for an evaluation period, this may be a natural and beneficial time to change tutors or students.

Number of Students to Be Tutored. After deciding on the subject area of tutoring and the amount of time tutoring will involve, the teacher needs to decide how many students are to participate. The total number of students will be a guideline for the number of tutors needed. At first the organizers of a program may want to limit the number of tutors they will train. As successful procedures are developed, another training program can be initiated for a second group of tutors. In a program with one-to-one tutoring, fifteen tutors is a manageable number with which to begin.

Extent of Teacher Involvement. Each teacher needs to know that his or her enthusiasm is important to the success of the program. While extensive participation is not necessary, teacher attention in the following areas is quite important:

1. showing interest in a student's work with the tutor.
2. showing appreciation to the tutor for his or her work.
3. being available to talk with the coordinator and/or tutor for scheduling, planning, and evaluating purposes.
4. assisting the tutor with instructional strategies that assure transfer of skills learned in tutoring to the classroom setting. For example, a teacher might prefer that a certain type of questioning sequence be used after the student reads a story. As the tutor and teacher work together, the chances of confusing the student are diminished.

In addition to basic support, some teachers may want to participate in the actual ongoing development of the program by assisting in screening and training, scheduling, or other administrative details. The range of teacher involvement varies, but teachers should always be assured that their ideas are valued and seriously considered in program development.

4 Recruiting and Selecting Tutors and Students

ORGANIZER

This chapter contains information about the recruitment and selection process for tutors and students.

If you are interested in:

- ideas for recruiting adults, see page 18.
- ideas about the interviewing of adult applicants, see page 22.
- recruiting in-school tutors, see page 24.
- information about selecting students to be tutored, see page 26.
- ways of preparing students to be tutored, see page 27.

THE first recruitment decision concerns the identification of a tutor population. If that population is to come from the student body of the school, recruitment is relatively straightforward. If the adult community is to be involved, recruitment is more complicated.

RECRUITING ADULT TUTORS

Don't let the complications make you shy away from adult populations. Adults who decide to tutor are particularly interested in working with children. Many have been parents or have cared for children and developed a natural way of relating to them. Adult tutors take their work seriously and understand its importance.

Persons from a variety of backgrounds can be tutors. Senior citizens, college students, and both working and nonworking parents should be considered. Adults can bring special skills to the tutoring activity. Those with hobbies such as photography, gardening, stamp-collecting and animal-training have much of interest to impart. Professions such as nursing, business, fire-fighting, and writing can add another dimension to tutoring programs.

Developing a Recruitment Strategy

Recruiting should start with the preparation of a message. Make your message as complete as possible (see figure 3). The more information given, the better people will know if they are interested in your tutoring program. That message can include such items as:

1. type of tutoring to be done, including ages of students and subject matter
2. amount of participation required

18

FIGURE 3 Sample Recruiting Message

Do you want to help?
BE A TUTOR
Serve as a volunteer tutor in
James Elem. School where students
are given help in math twice a week.
If you have a few morning hours per week
to share with a child
CALL James Elem. School
Washington and Flower
723-4950
We provide training.

---

3. place and time of tutoring activities
4. training opportunities
5. address and phone number of contact person

Once you have the basic elements of your message, focus on how you are going to present your information. Try to interest your audience. When speaking to groups, be sure to include examples where a tutor has made a difference in a student's work. Prepare written materials in an eye-catching way. You might consider the following ideas:

1. Give your program a name. Many schools call their programs "VIP—Volunteers in Public School," and volunteers wear a "VIP" button.
2. Use a slogan, such as "YOU HAVE SO MUCH TO GIVE—VOLUNTEER" or "ADOPT A SCHOOL."
3. Devise a drawing:

Reach Out.   Help a Child.

After the message is prepared, the method of dissemination must be determined. An ad in the paper, a notice sent home to parents, or a speech at a PTA meeting are some examples of dissemination methods. A variety of ways to advertise are shown in figure 4.

FIGURE 4 Ways to Advertise

1. Use of posters, brochures, and flyers
   a. These materials are easily made (see figure 3).
   b. Distribution of these materials depends on whom you want to encourage to volunteer. The following are a few placement ideas: install in grocery and drugstores, beauty parlors, barber shops, and apartment buildings; send home with children; give to high school students, churches, and so forth.

2. Newsletters
   a. Reach specific groups in this informal way. Use a small article or catchy advertisement. Try the newsletters in schools, businesses, churches, senior citizen organizations.

3. News media
   a. For a larger recruiting program, consider use of local radio, TV, and weekly and daily papers. Consider public service advertisements or a short story and/or captioned picture about your program.

4. Personal solicitations
   Use active tutors or other persons who know about the program to:
   a. Locate existing sources of volunteers. Look for your local volunteer bureau—locate this through the local health and welfare council, community chest, and chamber of commerce.
   b. Organize individual visits to neighbors.
   c. Give speeches to parent groups, citizen groups, junior and senior high school teachers (to recruit their students), and groups of interested older students (upper elementary through college).
   d. Help initiate a credit course for older students interested in tutoring.
   e. Telephone parents to solicit their interest.

An information form should also be prepared so that the volunteer will be able to provide information to the tutoring coordinator. Basic information about the tutor, such as address, phone number, education, special skills, job-related experiences, and time available for tutoring are types of information desired (see figure 5).

Once you have decided what population you are seeking, have developed a message, have determined a method of dissemination, and have drawn up an information form, you are well on your way to recruiting your first tutors.

FIGURE 5 Tutor Information Form

Date_____

Name_____

Address_____

Telephone (home)_____ (office)_____

Occupation_____

Employer's name_____

        address_____

How often do you want to tutor per week?_____

What days and times are convenient for you?

      Monday_____   Thursday_____
      Tuesday_____   Friday_____
      Wednesday_____   Saturday_____

Experience with children:

_____

_____

Special interests or skills that could be shared with children:

_____

_____

Do you have any preference as to the type of child with whom you want to work?

_____

_____

If you do not obtain the responses you had anticipated, reconsider your method of dissemination. It might be necessary to develop posters or brochures, to meet with civic and senior citizens' groups, to approach the news media, or to solicit the help of former tutors whom you know have contacts in the community.

Tutor Selection

Interviewing.   Personal interviews are a critical part of the re-cruitment procedure. Meetings with prospective tutors provide communication both ways. The tutors can obtain answers to their questions, and you can obtain necessary information and personal impressions of the tutors. The interviewer usually will have studied the tutor information form and therefore already knows some data. When information on the form is not clear, then the interview is the place to clarify it. You may also want to use an interview guide (see figure 6), which is designed to help the interviewer cover all important topics. Guides leave specific questions up to the interviewer, permitting a more personal approach. The following are basic interview procedures that should be followed:

1. Establish rapport with some prepared discussion stimu-lators.
2. Arrange for an informal setting. Don't sit behind a desk—it makes a person feel like an outsider.
3. Allow for the interviewee to ask questions, and try to answer as specifically as possible.
4. Have an interview guide from which you will ask ques-tions in order to obtain the information desired.
5. Have a planned way to conclude the interview in case it becomes extended beyond reason.
6. Take no notes during the interview, but write down as much as you can remember about each element of your interview guide as soon as possible afterward.

Choosing Tutors.   If you have in mind the characteristics needed for your program, you can select the best tutors from the group of volunteers. Desirable characteristics might include:

1. ability to relate to students
2. a friendly attitude toward the school program
3. possession of the necessary skills
4. commitment to see the project to completion
5. ability to work within your time constraints

FIGURE 6   Interview Guide

The following form indicates some of the areas the coordinator would likely cover in the initial interview of a tutor applicant.

Name of applicant _____

Address _____ Telephone _____

_____

Age _____ Sex _____ Occupation _____

1. Tutor strengths _____

_____

2. Tutor interests or hobbies _____

_____

3. Areas in which tutor would want to instruct _____

_____

4. Areas in which tutor would NOT want to instruct _____

_____

5. Age preference(s) _____

6. Tutor relatives in student population

	Name	Grade
	_____	____
	_____	____
	_____	____

7. Comments: _____

_____

_____	_____
Interviewer	Date

Depending upon your objectives, other characteristics can be added. Be certain that you communicate that certain characteristics are needed for this particular tutoring program.

Rejecting Tutor Applicants.   It is important to realize that you may get responses from persons who for some reason are not suited for the tutoring you have planned. Fifty volunteers may respond when you only need twenty. A volunteer may not have worked well in the school on prior occasions. Some may want to do their "own thing," and that "thing" may not happen to fit into your tutoring objectives. You must be prepared to reject these volunteers in a way that does not strain your public relations and leaves the door open for the volunteer to be involved at another time.

IN-SCHOOL RECRUITING

Tutors from within a school can come from two sources: within the student's classroom and from grades above. Cross-grade tutoring generally involves older students tutoring younger ones. With cross-age tutoring, attention must be paid to all of the logistics involved when there are two teachers and two students, each missing classroom instruction during the tutoring period.

Peer-tutoring involves two students of the same age working together for a specific reason. It can be very informal and even spontaneous. One student needs to have sight words reinforced, so the teacher assigns a second student to help. Another student needs extra practice on a spelling lesson, so someone helps out. Most of the suggestions that follow are directed toward cross-age tutoring because it involves more coordination.

Recruiting from the school population is fairly straightforward since you know the students and have ready access to them (see Appendix G for a sample recruitment plan). However, several considerations need to be given to in-school recruiting.

A recruiting message and an information form should be worked out (see "Developing a Recruitment Strategy," earlier in this chapter). Posters that highlight the accomplishments of the tutoring program and mention of the school activities related to a tutoring club are strong enticements to participate.

Teachers who provide the tutor population need to be involved in the planning so that tutors do not forgo essential

Peer-tutoring involves two students of the same age working together for a specific reason.

instruction. Nothing undermines a program faster than a teacher who resents a student's missing instruction. Tutoring must be seen as an important in-school learning activity.

Capable students are an obvious choice to become tutors. They offer the necessary skills and can afford to miss some classwork. But experience has demonstrated that all types of students profit from the tutoring experience. The following are examples of the range of students who might succeed as tutors:

1. Slow-learning fifth graders are often seen as quite capable by second graders. In this situation the tutor preparation is a "real" educational activity that the tutors accept with enthusiasm. As they obtain positive feedback from the second graders, the self-esteem of these tutors grows, especially since they have not previously experienced great success in school.

2.   The class bully or discipline problem can be offered a tutor-
     ing opportunity. Such students often take the responsibility
     seriously, with a corresponding improvement in their be-
     havior.
3.   Students from the middle of ability groups often are over-
     looked, but they can be fine tutors and need the resulting
     feelings of success as much as other types of students do.
4.   Students with skills such as artistic talent or athletic ability
     can provide very special tutoring needs.

When selecting in-school tutors, try to give every volunteer a
chance sometime during the year, but do not force a reluctant
student to become a tutor. The program will only succeed if the
tutors are enthusiastic and serious about their tutoring responsibilities.

Schedules must be worked out and regularly followed, and
tutoring space provided. If a teacher provides four tutors for a
half hour, make sure they are back in their rooms inside that half
hour. In-school tutors must always work under supervision, so
working areas must be established in places where supervision is
possible.

Recruitment of tutors is an exciting and a rewarding experience. Plan it well and enjoy it.

SELECTING AND PREPARING STUDENTS FOR TUTORING

The Selection Process

Selecting those to be tutored is an important step in developing a
good tutoring program. Many if not all students in a given school
population could profit from tutoring, so all types of students
should be considered, including:

1.   talented and gifted students who need direction in their
     independent study
2.   students with skill deficiencies
3.   average students who need some individual attention
4.   students who have missed lessons due to absence
5.   students with special interests such as art, music, or
     woodworking

The type of tutors available will influence the type of students to be tutored. Peer-tutoring can be arranged more easily than cross-age or adult tutoring, since it is usually done when the classroom teacher is present. Students in need of peer-tutoring can be identified informally and matched with those students possessing the specific skills required. Tutors from the community may wish to utilize special skills or qualifications such as speaking another language, membership in certain professions, or artistic talents, in their tutoring; the students chosen should share those interests.

The classroom teacher should be directly involved in the selection of students. The teacher's input will help assure a cooperative atmosphere in which the tutor can work most efficiently. Without such support, the program cannot succeed.

Parents must also be involved. If a child announces at home that he played games with Jamie Wright during spelling class, a parent protest that immediately puts the program coordinator and teacher on the defensive is likely. This can be avoided, and parental support generated, by sending home an announcement of the program requesting parents to indicate their desire to have their child involved. A parent consent form for tutoring is found in Appendix A.

Finally, at times the students to be tutored will be involved in the selection process. Chances for success are increased if students volunteer to be tutored, although they may be asked to try a tutoring experience to become aware of what it can do for them. In many cases they want to continue the activity. If not, others can take their place.

Disappointment can occur when a student volunteers to be tutored but for some reason is not selected. The reason for the nonselection should be made clear to the student and, if possible, a commitment should be made to involve the student in the near future.

Preparation for Tutoring

The teacher and the coordinator need to prepare the students for tutoring once they are selected. They should know who the tutor will be, when and where tutoring will take place, how long it will last, how it will affect the instruction that they will miss, and what the advantages are for them. Guidelines for behavior during tutoring should also be discussed. Questions and concerns need to be met before tutoring starts as well as during the program.

To provide the tutor with essential information, the teacher should also prepare an information form for each student. A sample of this type of form is shown in figure 7.

FIGURE 7 Student Information Form
(To Be Filled Out by the Teacher)

Teacher

Room number

Student's name _____

Age _____ Sex _____ Room number _____

Grade/Level _____

Subject area in which tutoring is desired

_____

_____

Special information (interests, specific personality features)

_____

_____

Parental permission obtained   Yes_____ No_____

Time most convenient for teacher to talk about this student

_____

Other comments:

_____

_____

5 Administration of a Tutoring Program

ORGANIZER

This chapter contains suggestions for making administrative arrangements so a tutoring program can operate efficiently and effectively.
If you are interested in:

- finding space for tutoring, see page 30.
- information about the assignment of tutors to students, see page 30.
- establishing procedures for the operation of a tutoring program, see page 32.

ORGANIZING for tutoring involves making the necessary arrangements so tutors and students can work comfortably together without disrupting the general school routine. The major tasks are to find a suitable place for tutoring, assign tutors to students, and devise operating procedures so the program will run smoothly.

FINDING SPACE FOR TUTORING

Tutoring has been conducted in a variety of places. Lunchrooms, hallways, libraries, and resource rooms have all been successfully used. Since many schools do not have extra unused rooms, the coordinator must sometimes be quite resourceful and squeeze tutors into corners when space is available. The space, however, should be bright, pleasant, and conducive to learning. It may be necessary to schedule tutoring only on days when certain teaching specialists are not in the school so their rooms can be used, or when the librarian or media specialist does not hold regular classes. If a teacher is coordinating a program, then this person's classroom may be an appropriate place for tutoring.

ASSIGNMENT OF TUTORS

Many pieces of information are needed before tutors can be assigned.

Teachers should provide:

1. the names of students to be tutored and any special information about them that might be pertinent to pairing. (This is an appropriate time to collect the student information forms.)
2. times that students can be tutored. By asking participating teachers for weekly schedules, you will know when special classes are held and be able to schedule around them.

    3.   their suggestions about the length and frequency of tutoring sessions.

✗ Tutors should provide:

    1.   the days and times that are most convenient for them.
    2.   the number of times per week they want to work.
    3.   their preferences, if any, for the sex, age, or personality types of their students. If they relate particularly well to aggressive or shy children or have special hobbies or interests, encourage them to share this information. (The tutor information form should have all this information. See figure 5 on page 21.)

Decisions for assigning tutors to students are based on a number of criteria. The times that tutors and students are available for tutoring are a basic consideration. When you review this information, accessibility to places for tutoring should also be considered. In addition to the practical consideration of time, special tutor, teacher, or student preferences and interests are extremely important. If there is a question about a certain pairing, the tutor or the teacher should be consulted. Occasionally additional students or tutors should enter the program to suit particular interests and needs.

In programs that use students as tutors, pairing has been done randomly and by race, sex, and achievement. The purposes of the program, however, can alter the criteria for pairing students. Lippitt (1969) suggests an age difference of three or more years between students if emphasis is to be placed on the tutor-student relationship. She suggests that this age difference allows younger students to receive help without having to compare their skills with those of their tutors. It is normally important for the tutor to feel older.

Anyone familiar with the tutors and students involved can easily do tutor-student pairing. In schools where tutors are assigned to teachers rather than to individual students, the coordinator simply assigns the tutors to the teachers who do the pairing. In situations where tutors are not working with one particular teacher, however, the coordinator is in the best position to supervise the pairing of tutors and students.

Once tutors have been assigned, each assignment should be checked with the tutor and teacher to see if the arrangement still meets their schedules. A written confirmation of tutoring times and days should also be given to tutor, teacher, and student. This written confirmation could be the same master schedule that is posted in the school for interested personnel (figure 8) or an individual form for each person (figure 9).

ESTABLISHING PROCEDURES

A carefully planned program allows participants to know what is expected of them. The following are a few crucial areas that need special attention.

Developing a Central Information Center.   This center may be a small bulletin board in a hall or a room where tutors go on a regular basis each time they come into the school. All written information can be posted here. A copy of the master tutoring schedule should be available as well as a calendar with all school holidays, class trips, testing days, assemblies, and so forth. By checking the calendar on a regular basis, tutors will be aware of any recent schedule changes. This bulletin board is also a place for general notices of meetings; posting of new and old general school procedures, such as where to park or what to do in an emergency; or anything else that may be of interest to tutors. In addition, some schools have individual mailboxes for tutors (file folders or milk cartons stapled together).

Attendance.   Because tutors are in a responsible teaching position, the school needs to know when they are in the school and when they are absent. Many schools have the tutors sign in regularly upon arrival. When a tutor is going to be absent, he or she is asked to let the teacher and/or coordinator know as soon as possible. Since teachers and students generally look forward to the arrival of the tutors and plan their schedules accordingly, they may be upset when tutors do not arrive on time. If a tutor is to be absent for an extended period, arrangements need to be made for the student. Another tutor may work with two students

FIGURE 8 Farmland High School Weekly Tutoring Schedule

Tutor/Student	Monday	Tuesday	Wednesday	Thursday	Friday
Carrie James/ Robin Jones	9:00–9:30 Media Center		9:00–9:30 Media Center		9:00–9:30 Media Center
Jeri Stewart/ Carolyn Brown		1:00–1:30 Art Room		9:30–10:00 Art Room	
Sharon Vale/ Joan White	10:00–10:45 Cafeteria		10:00–10:45 Cafeteria	10:00–10:45 Cafeteria	
Victor Pico/ John Salz	1:00–1:45 Spanish Room			1:00–1:45 Media Center	1:00–1:45 Media Center
Tyrone Cohan/ Lenny Gatewood			1:00–1:45 Spanish Room	1:00–1:45 Book Room	
Rebecca Villa/ Frank Loy		10:30–11:00 Art Room		10:30–11:00 Art Room	
Joan Collishaw/ Judy Bird	9:30–10:45 Media Center		9:30–10:45 Media Center		9:30–10:45 Media Center
John Gambrell/ Jane Bryant			2:00–2:45 Spanish Room		
Larry Birch/ Vincent Raywood	10:00–10:45 Book Room	10:00–10:45 Book Room		10:00–10:45 Book Room	
Jason Jackson/ Miles Rubin	1:00–1:45 Spanish Room		1:00–1:45 Spanish Room	1:00–1:45 Media Center	
Valeria Flood/ Honey Green	2:00–2:45 Media Center		2:00–2:45 Media Center		2:00–2:45 Media Center

PLEASE CIRCLE YOUR TUTORING TIME AFTER YOU TUTOR.

at one time, or a list of substitute tutors can be compiled for these special situations. Tutors also need to be informed of times when students will not be available. Student absences generally cannot be predicted, but all other schedule changes need to be communicated to tutors in advance. Tutors begin to feel quite unappreciated if they repeatedly arrive only to find their students on a trip or at an assembly that had been previously planned.

FIGURE 9   Individual Schedule

Tutor	Mrs. Janet Berry
Student	Nancy Slim
Grade	5
Teacher	Mrs. Jean Barrio
Day(s) and times	M (T) W (TH) F S 10:00–10:30
Place	Cafeteria

Use of School Materials and Equipment.   Most schools have an array of equipment and materials that can be used by tutors with a minimum of training. This training, however, is very important to assure that the equipment is properly maintained. As tutors become familiar with the school, they can be encouraged to use the available materials. They need to be given such information as which material they can use, where to check it in and out, and how to use it. Careful attention to these orientation procedures can help prevent loss and misuse due to the inexperience of the user.

Providing Space for Tutors.   In progams where the tutors are coming from the community to work in the schools, space must be provided for personal belongings and for meetings between tutoring sessions. If tutors can informally gather, have refreshments, and get to know each other, they become more comfortable with the school, establish friendships, and exchange ideas. This exchange is one of the most effective types of tutor-training. In some schools it is difficult to find space for socializing. The teachers' room is often ideal if it is not already overcrowded and if the teachers feel positively about the tutoring program. A lunchroom area or a counselor's suite may also be appropriate. Any room or corner that can be made comfortable is sufficient.

Creating a System for Expressing Concerns.   It must be clear from the beginning who is in charge of the tutoring program. Tutors and school personnel should know that they can go to the coordinator with any problem or question, no matter how small. If an atmosphere of concern and trust is developed early in the program, small concerns can be voiced and dealt with quickly and efficiently. If, however, tutors do not feel comfortable asking questions, small concerns may accumulate and turn into larger problems. In order to encourage tutors and teachers to bring up their questions, the coordinator needs to be accessible as well as friendly. This entails having frequent and regular office hours and making telephone calls to follow up on messages. If the coordinator will not be available for a time, a substitute who can make decisions and handle problems should be clearly designated. The coordinator also needs to determine when the students' teachers are available for conferences about students. This schedule will ensure that tutors do not interrupt classes.

6 Organizing Tutor-Training

ORGANIZER

This chapter presents information about the need for tutor-training and discusses areas that should be considered when organizing and planning an initial training program.

If you are interested in:

- the rationale for tutor-training, see page 38.
- information regarding the specific details that should be considered when organizing and planning initial tutor-training, see page 38.

IS TRAINING REALLY NECESSARY?

Many of the early tutoring programs varied in the extent to which they trained tutors. While no research results give definitive guidelines for training, work in the last fifteen years stresses its necessity (Koskinen, 1975; Devin-Sheehan, Feldman and Allen, 1976). Some training programs concentrate heavily on the relationship between tutor and student, while others spend considerable time on background information in the specific subject area of tutoring. Regardless of the major emphasis of the training, tutors need to know what is expected of them, and they must be given guidelines. While the extent of training may vary according to the complexity of the tutoring tasks and the previous experience of the tutors, initial training should be complete enough to make the tutors feel confident. Additional guidance and training are usually needed while the tutoring program is in progress.

CONSIDERATIONS FOR AN INITIAL TRAINING PROGRAM

The first training sessions are important since they often set the tutors' impressions for the work to follow. Several areas should be considered.

Initial Welcome.   It is vital to help tutors feel welcome and at ease. The training program should be held in comfortable surroundings. Name tags should be provided to enable people to begin to learn each other's names. Making refreshments available will help to relax those present and contribute to positive feelings about the program. Opening remarks that include the school's appreciation for the tutors' interest are just another way of letting the tutors know they are valued.

Background Information.   When people come to a new situation, they become comfortable faster if they can obtain relevant

38

information. Of interest is the background of the students, staff, and neighborhood and types of school programs in progress. Tutors should be given a list of staff names and a map of the school, and they also benefit from a brief history of the tutoring program, including how long it has operated, the number and types of people who have participated, and the subject areas of tutoring.

Goals of Tutoring. A discussion of the goals of the program helps to orient tutors. One school presented goals to tutors as a summary of why the program was developed. The goals chosen were to help students feel positively about themselves, enjoy their schoolwork, and increase their skill in word recognition. It was clear at the outset of this program that helping children feel good about themselves was as important as developing skill in word recognition.

Overview of Tutoring. At the beginning of the training session, it is also helpful to outline all aspects of the total program. This allows the tutor to anticipate future events and understand the scope of the program. One school's overview presented the following points:

1. initial training—three sessions of one and one half hours each to help prepare for tutoring. These sessions include ideas for working with students.
2. tutoring—working with a student two times a week for eight weeks including:
   - picking the student up from class
   - playing math computation games with the student
   - assisting student with math homework
   - taking the student back to class after a twenty-minute session
3. ongoing training—attending weekly meetings with other tutors to talk about teaching experiences.

Behavior of an Effective Tutor. A description of the qualities that make people effective tutors can give potential tutors guidelines for their own behavior. But such a list is quite extensive, and it may not mean much to tutors if these qualities are simply enumerated. Instead, tutors might be asked what qualities they think are important, and then a list that reflects the ideas of the whole group can be developed. Some points to include if they are not suggested by the tutors are:

- reliable (comes to tutoring regularly and on time)
- helps students feel good about themselves
  —by accepting them as they are
  —by giving supportive responses
- prepares instructional materials oriented toward student interests
- flexible (adjusts to school changes)
- respects rights of school personnel (supportive of teacher)
- respects confidential information about students and schools

When working with student tutors, it is important to discuss the honor and responsibility that are associated with the position. A "Student Tutor Agreement" (see figure 10) can be given

FIGURE 10   Student Tutor Agreement

It is agreed that _____ will be a student tutor during the months of March, April, and May.

It is further agreed that the above-named student tutor will execute his/her duties to the best of his/her ability. These duties will include planning for tutoring, helping his/her student with activities, and attending weekly tutoring meetings.

Continued participation in the tutoring program is contingent upon the interest of the student tutor and approval of participating staff members of_____ _____Elementary School.

Approved by:

Student tutor _____

Classroom teacher _____

Program coordinator _____

Principal _____

Date _____

---

them to explain the role that the tutor will have. It may also be important to discuss the meaning of "responsibility." Tutors can suggest things they can do to show how they would be responsible (leaving and returning to their classes on time, walking quietly in the halls, courteously picking up their students, planning activities *before* the tutoring session). At the end of the training program, the student tutors can decide if they still want to undertake their assignments. If they have the consent of their teachers and the coordinator, then they can assume the responsibility of tutors.

Some programs have also successfully used contracts with adult tutors. While very brief and informal, these contracts help emphasize that a tutor should be a responsible member of the school community (see figure 11).

FIGURE 11   Adult Tutor Contract

It is agreed that _____ will be a tutor from _____ to _____. It is further agreed that the position of tutor involves working with students, respecting confidential information, and being a responsible member of the school community.

Approved by:

Tutor _____

Program coordinator _____

Principal _____

Date _____

Determining Student Interests.   Tutors can easily learn to determine students' interests. This activity will help them begin their initial sessions and also provide a basis for many future discussions and activities. Tutors can use a prepared interest inventory or develop a list of their own questions. If they make up their own, it initiates the questioning process and shows them they can easily think of many pertinent things to ask. If tutors share their questions, a homemade interest inventory is quickly developed.

FIGURE 12   Student Interest Inventory

1. Do you like films or TV? What do you like to watch?
2. What kinds of sports do you like to play?
3. Do you like animals? What kinds?
4. What kinds of books or magazines do you like to read?
5. What do you want to be when you grow up?
6. Do you have any brothers or sisters?
7. What do you like to do in your spare time?
8. What do you like about school? What don't you like about school?
9. What is your favorite musical group?

Figure 12 shows a list of questions developed by a group of fifth grade tutors. These tutors chose four of the questions to be used at their first sessions.

Because students are also curious about their tutors, tutors should freely share their common interests or other special things that they like. It is particularly enjoyable if they bring in things to show students (such as a stamp or coin collection). This sharing can mark the beginning of a relationship. If a small part of each tutoring session is devoted to talking about personal interests, the bond of friendship will continue to grow.

Subject Matter Knowledge.   As discussed earlier, tutoring can be done in all subject areas and with a variety of methods and materials. In many programs tutors make their own materials, while in others they might be given programmed material and asked to follow it exactly. Whatever the procedure, tutors need to be trained carefully so they know specifically what to do in the subject area and how to make it meaningful for the student.

Little research information discusses the amount of initial training that tutors should have. Since it is generally not feasible to offer a full course in the subject matter to be taught, it is vital to start with clearly defined tasks that both tutors and students can successfully complete. As tutors gain experience and receive more training, increasingly complex activities can be handled.

Initial training that includes practice of the type of task to be done is especially valuable. Not only can this practice, in a controlled situation where advice is available, build tutor confidence, but it is also a way of working out problems a tutor may have. Specific examples of instructional activities for tutor-training can be found in chapter 7.

Planning Tutoring Sessions. Planning is an essential ingredient of successful tutoring. While preparation for tutoring takes less time as tutors become more familiar with their situations, even experienced instructors still allow time for planning before each session. This must be explained to tutors. After familiarizing themselves with the material to be used or designing materials appropriate for their students' needs, tutors also must consider how best to present the information. Tutors can be encouraged to include at least the following elements in each session:

1. help the student feel at ease (talk about an interest or something that is happening at school or at home)
2. work with a specific activity
3. discuss with the students
   • their reactions to the present activity
   • the plans for the next session

This format was successfully used with tutors who were given a logbook of planning forms that were to be completed before and after each session (see figure 13). This log served both as a planning book and an evaluation form. By keeping a record of what happened at each session, tutors could follow up on successful ideas or adapt lessons as a result of previous experience.

Another type of record-keeping format is shown in figure 14. This report can be as brief or complete as the tutor desires and often will contain pertinent evaluation information to be used for future planning. As can be seen in figure 14, the tutor has planned the lesson for February 9 as a result of information from the previous lesson. Regardless of the type of record-keeping to be done, daily plans should be kept so they can be used for continuous evaluation, and so tutors, students, and teachers can see how much has been accomplished.

FIGURE 13 Tutoring Log

Name _Anita_   Date _March 4_

Plans

1. Help student feel at ease.
2. Activity _" Bingo " game with 20 words. Copying new words to make the " fish " game._
3. Other activities (planned or unplanned) _Reading Frog and Toad Together._

Comments on Tutoring Session (things that happened, successes, problems, ideas for future sessions)

Anita really enjoys playing board games. She knows 12 words well. She asked to play " Candy Land " with more words next time. She didn't want to read the book, so I read 4 pages and she read one.

How do you feel about your tutoring session?

Anita was tired but perked up with " Bingo." The session was better than last time.

Working in the School. Tutors need specific information about the schools in which they will be working. The following areas need to be considered but will depend on school policies for the specifics of their content.

1. *Understanding the School Program.* To help tutors understand how their efforts fit into the total instructional program, the staff should provide an overview of the school program. This overview should include instructional objectives, principal methods and materials, and resources available to teachers. The instructional overview is particularly

FIGURE 14   Notes from a Tutoring Log

Name: *John*

Date	Topic	Comments
Feb. 6	Review 5 and 6 multiplication tables. Use flash cards with football games.	Knew most of the 5 tables. Needs a review of 6×6, 7, 8, 9. Loves the games — wants more sports games with basketball and soccer.
Feb. 9	Review a few 5 problems as an encouraging warm-up; then play a basketball game with 6 and 7 tables.	Still needs work with the late 6 tables. Need to use some counting beans in the near future.

important if the tutoring is designed as a portion of an Individualized Educational Program (IEP). The tutor in these cases should have specific information about the objectives and strategies of the entire IEP.

2. *Understanding Discipline and Management Procedures.*   Most schools have developed rules for student behavior. Tutors need to understand those rules and know their role regarding enforcement. Management procedures for dealing with groups of students must also be understood.

3. *Understanding Communication Systems.*   Tutors should be aware of appropriate communications systems with students, teachers, and other school staff. This involves knowing who is in charge, how and when to approach others, and sensitivity to the thoughts of others. Nonverbal communication should also be stressed.

Tutors also need to be given the administrative procedures that have been developed by the school staff (see chapter 5). These procedures should be put in writing and be carefully explained to each of the tutors. (A sample form that can be given to tutors is shown in figure 15.) A few areas that can be included are:

1. *Schedules and Related Information.*   Procedures developed for alerting tutors to schedules and adjustments in schedules, school news, and other matters must be described to them. Copies of their assignment schedules with the names of students, their teachers, and the times and places of tutoring should be given to the tutors (see figures 8 and 9). A visit to the place where all tutor-related information is posted can help emphasize the importance of checking the calendar or schedule sheet for changes or noting meeting dates.

FIGURE 15   Administrative Procedures of the Larksburg Tutoring Program

---

Schedule Arrangements

All schedule arrangements, announcements of meetings, and so forth will be posted on the bulletin board in the counselor's suite.

BE SURE TO CHECK THE BOARD *DAILY.*

Attendance

1. Coming to school regularly and on time is *so important.* If, however, you cannot come for tutoring, tell, call, or write to those in charge *before* tutoring.

   CONTACT: Gladys Knight—723–6842 or 667–5767 (home)
   or
   Jim Hamble—723–8642 (eighth grade teacher)
   or
   Your students' teachers

2. Sign in each time you come to tutoring. The sign-in sheet is in the office.

3. Check the school calendar and with your students so you can anticipate the dates the students will not be available for tutoring.

Using School Materials and Equipment

Check with Gladys Knight for supplies. Nancy Kane, the reading teacher, also has supplies when needed in a hurry.

FIGURE 15 (continued)

Use only the equipment you have been trained to use by a Larksburg staff member (machines have individual differences too!). Jeri Landon, the media specialist, can be asked for advice on training. Gladys, Jim, and Nancy can also help.

Materials should be *signed out* from the media center.

Use of the Teachers' Room

You are welcome in most parts of the building at any time. If, however, you want to sit as a group and talk, the teachers' room (next to the media center) is particularly comfortable. Coffee or tea can be bought for a 15¢ donation.

Expressing Concerns

If you have a question, or problem—*no matter how small*—go to Gladys Knight. Especially good times for her at school are 8:30–9:30, 11:45–1:00, 2:45–3:30. Also feel free to call her at home (667–5767) after 8:00 PM. If Gladys is not available, see Jim Hamble in Room 206 or Nancy Kane in Room 102.

Find out from Gladys when are convenient times to talk to your students' teachers about questions.

General School Procedures

1. Tutors can dress casually but professionally, as teachers do.
2. Parking can be found on the streets around the school. The few spaces behind the school are for the administrative staff.
3. In case of fire, take your students out to the street by way of the *nearest safe exit.*
4. In case of a health emergency, go immediately to Mrs. Wilder, the secretary, in the main office.
5. All information you have about your students should be kept *confidential.*
6. Permission for trips should be obtained from Gladys Knight.

---

2. *Attendance.* Attendance procedures can be discussed with tutors in conjunction with what to do when an absence is expected. If tutors know that teachers and students are waiting for them, they are more concerned about coming to school regularly and on time. The names of people to call, write, or talk to about a forthcoming absence should be given to each tutor. The need to check the school and class schedules for days students might be absent should also be stressed.

3. *Use of School Materials and Equipment.* Tutors should be advised where to get supplies, and these should be available before tutoring begins. Also, to avoid confusion, the procedure for use of equipment and commercial materials must be carefully outlined.

4. *Where to Go When Not Tutoring.* In programs where tutors come from the community, it is helpful to take them on a tour of the school including designated areas where they can rest and socialize.

5. *Expressing Concerns.* Tutors should know the names of the coordinator or substitutes to contact when a problem arises. It is helpful if they also know times that are particularly convenient for the coordinator. Tutors also need to know when they can contact teachers without interrupting their classes.

6. *General School Procedures.* Every school has a number of rules and regulations of which people working there should be aware. Emergency procedures, permission for trips, handling of confidential information, dress code, and parking arrangements are a few areas that could be discussed with tutors.

Creating a Climate for Learning—Continuous Evaluation. Individual factors that help create a positive climate for learning have been discussed in the initial training program, but it is helpful to pull them all together for the tutors and to briefly review them. Even though the tutors only work with students for a short time each week, they can still develop a relationship that encourages learning. In anticipating the tutor's arrival, the student knows whether it will be an exciting, productive time or whether it is just a chance to get out of class and fool around. When evaluating each individual session, tutors might consider:

Did I

- come on time and was I well prepared?
- spend time talking to the students about their interests apart from the tutoring topic?

- provide meaningful activities that were of interest to the students?
- prepare the students for the activity?
- provide time for them to discuss their reactions to the activity?
- know the school's rules and routines so I could reinforce them?
- give encouragement and praise for the things the students did well?

An evaluation of the student's interest and progress in relationship to the tutor's behavior can provide important information for future planning. This information can be used as a starting point for the development of strategies to make tutoring even more effective.

7 Sample Instructional Activities for Tutor-Training

ORGANIZER

This chapter contains sample activities for consideration in tutor-training. On the next page, each topic is listed and its page number is identified. Select the topics of interest to you and your program.

SINCE every tutoring program should be developed to meet the needs of its students, tutor trainers will want to select the most appropriate instructional activities for their programs. This chapter provides tutor trainers with ideas and suggests resources.

The first section presents a teaching plan that can be used with the general tutoring strategies described in the second section. These strategies can be used in most types of tutoring. The purpose of each is explained, and brief suggestions for teaching are included so the strategy can be given to tutors in the format presented. The third section offers teaching plans for a series of specific tutoring strategies. Tutor trainers will be able to select and adapt ideas from this section according to the needs of their individual programs. A teaching plan for dealing with common problems that tutors face is presented in the final section.

TEACHING PLAN FOR GENERAL TUTORING STRATEGIES

Objective.   To acquaint tutors with general tutoring strategies that are needed for most types of tutoring.

Procedures
1.   Review the general tutoring strategies discussed on the following pages. Select a few to introduce at each training session. The strategies presented in this section are in a format suitable for use directly with tutors.
2.   Have a brief discussion about the importance of the particular strategy. For example, when introducing "Focusing on the Strengths of Students," you might discuss the need for a positive self-concept and the danger of being overly critical. Use examples from the real world of your tutors.
3.   Provide specific examples of how tutors can use the strategy in their work.
4.   Encourage tutors to think of other examples that relate to

their own past experiences. Tutors can develop these ideas by brainstorming as a group or working in pairs.

5.   When possible, provide tutors with written examples of how to use the strategy in their work with students. These examples can be suggested by the tutors themselves or can have been presented to them in the training session. This written information can be very helpful to tutors when they are planning their sessions.

Resource Material

Canfield, Jack, and Wells, Harold C. *100 Ways to Enhance Self-Concept in the Classroom.* Englewood Cliffs: Prentice-Hall, 1976.

Carin, Arthur A., and Sund, Robert B. *Developing Questioning Techniques: A Self-Concept Approach.* Columbus, Ohio: Charles E. Merrill, 1971.

Gambrell, Linda B., and Wilson, Robert M. *Focusing on the Strengths of Children.* Belmont, Calif.: Fearon, 1973.

Glasser, William. *The Effect of School Failure on the Life of the Child.* Washington, D.C.: National Association of Elementary School Principals, National Education Association, 1971.

Mager, Robert F. *Developing Attitude Toward Learning.* Belmont, Calif.: Fearon, 1968.

Randolph, Norma, and Howe, William. *Self Enhancing Education.* Palo Alto, Calif.: Stanford University Press, 1966.

Russell, David H., and Russell, Elizabeth F. *Listening Aids Through the Grades.* Revised by Dorothy Grant Hennings. 2d ed. New York: Teachers College Press, 1979.

Tanner, Laurel N. *Classroom Discipline for Effective Teaching and Learning.* New York: Holt, Rinehart and Winston, 1978.

GENERAL TUTORING STRATEGIES

Focusing on the Strengths of Students

Objective.   To help students feel good about themselves as learners.

Explanation.   Many students who need the help of a tutor do not feel good about themselves. They do not feel that they can learn things easily. Sometimes this perception is the result of the group instruction that teachers must use. The pace of the instruction leaves certain students behind, and they get poor grades on papers and report cards. By focusing on strengths, tutors can change those negative feelings to positive ones. The following suggestions are examples of ways a tutor can focus on strengths.

Suggestions

1. Mark correct answers on student papers—not incorrect ones.
2. When grading a paper, indicate the number correct, not the number wrong.
3. Write personal notes to your students about observed behavior that you would like to reinforce.
4. Write notes to the students' teachers and parents when they do well.
5. Create an award letter that indicates the successful completion of a contract, project, or assignment. For example, see figure 16.
6. Develop progress charts that indicate the number of successes—words learned, assignments completed, questions answered. For example, see figure 17.

FIGURE 16   Student Award

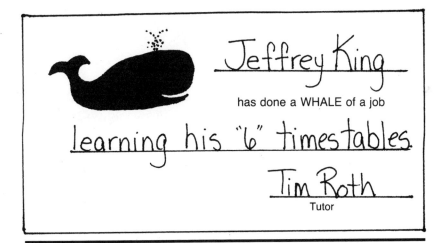

FIGURE 17 Progress Chart

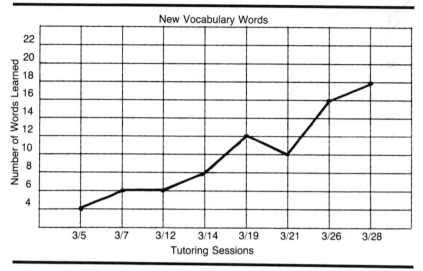

Working with Student Interests

Objective. To make tutoring sessions interesting for the students.

Explanation. Some students find much of what goes on in school to be boring. As a tutor you have a chance to change that. If you can make lessons interesting, then you will have an attentive, interested student with whom to work.

Suggestions
1. Determine things that interest your students. Ask about interests in sports, TV, books, and other things. Make note of these interests immediately after your sessions so that you will remember them.
2. Plan to use something from the list of interests in as many lessons as possible. For example, if a student likes dogs, then plan to read a story about dogs or collect some dog pictures from magazines and share them.
3. Watch for changing interests. Sports interests, for example, can change when a season is over. It is important not to

overdo an emphasis on a given interest. By paying attention to your students' responses, you can usually tell when an interest is declining.

4. Talk with your students' teachers about what you are doing with interests. Teachers usually have good ideas about how to utilize a student's interests.

Listening to Students

Objective.   To let students know you are interested in what they have to say.

Explanation.   What students say is important to them. Many students report that they do not feel that their teachers listen to them. When that feeling persists, communication is hampered. Students begin to feel that what they say is not valued.

Suggestions
1. Be certain to look at your students when they are talking to you.
2. Use your body to show you are listening carefully. At times you might nod your head in agreement, smile, gesture with your hands, or lean forward with your body to indicate your sincere interest.
3. Try to understand the full intent of the message being sent to you. At times the words will suggest meanings that cannot be stated. For example, a student might be saying, "I need your help" but might be feeling, "I'm dumb."
4. Hear students out. At times students are interrupted before they have completed their thoughts. Such interruptions indicate that their ideas are not valued.

Responding to Your Students

Objective.   To encourage students and help them feel accepted by the way you respond to them.

Explanation.   Each time we respond to something that students say or do, we are giving them information about our feelings. It is important to know what you are communicating when you respond to students.

Suggestions

1. It helps to provide encouragement when things are not going well. Comments such as, "Let's try that again. I'll help you," tend to make students feel like persevering.

2. When their achievements are recognized, students can be encouraged to continue trying. For example, acknowledge the eight words spelled correctly instead of the two that are missed. Of course you will need to deal with the two misspellings, but only after you recognize the correctly spelled words.

3. Attempt to keep eye contact. Eye contact is one way to promote sincerity as you respond to your students.

4. Try to respond without being evaluative. Discussion and disagreement need not be conducted in terms that make the students feel "wrong."

5. Think of different ways to tell your students they have done a good job. Try comments such as:
    • What a great answer!
    • Excellent! That was a difficult problem!
    • You really remembered a lot!
    • Good thinking!
    • I like the way you did that!

6. Try to communicate by your responses that you enjoy working with your students. Smiles, nods, and pleasant voice tones all indicate your enjoyment.

Helping Students Pay Attention

Objective.   To assist students in concentrating on their learning activities.

Explanation.   Most of the activities involving learning require students to concentrate thoroughly. We call this *attention to task.* We have all experienced difficulty concentrating on a task, and we realize that we have not learned what we set out to do. Tutors can try some activities to help their students attend to the tasks they have planned.

Suggestions
1. Plan activities for short periods of time. Working with sight vocabulary for half an hour would be boring for most students. A ten-minute lesson might not be.
2. Share your time plan with your students. If a part of a session is to be for ten minutes, then tell them. Many students will react favorably when they know that attention to a given task is expected for a short period of time.
3. Make certain that students know when they are finished. Some students view school as a never-ending series of activities. Set up your activities so that students will know what must be done to complete the task.
4. Let students know that you care about their attention to task. Send a note to their teachers when it has been good.
5. Have your students self-evaluate their attention to task. They might be given a rating sheet, and they can circle how well they did. For example, Today, I worked:
    • very well
    • well
    • not too well
    If they self-evaluate "well" or "not too well," then you can ask them why. Many times they will explain their lack of attention to task in such a way that you can make adjustments. Students appreciate such adjustments. It shows them that you care about them as learners.

Helping Students Complete Assignments Independently

Objective.   To prepare students to complete assignments independently.

Explanation.   Many students work well under teacher direction but find it difficult to complete assignments on their own. It is common for students in tutoring programs to ask their tutors for help with assignments.

Suggestions

1. When students ask for help, first try to determine ways in which they might help themselves. For example, if they ask for the spelling of a word, suggest that they use a dictionary or try to spell it on their own. Independence is the final objective.
2. Help students see when their assignments are completed. Set some goals that can be achieved. If the assignment is lengthy, set goals for sections of it.
3. Help develop the habit of checking assignments before turning them in to the teacher. Again, set goals for self-checking. For example, students might ask themselves:
   • Are words spelled correctly?
   • Is the assignment neat in appearance?
   • Is the assignment complete?
4. Help students use resources within the school. Go with them to the library and show how useful the card catalog can be.
5. Once you have helped a student with an assignment, try to obtain feedback from the teacher. Determine if your effort was helpful and if you need to help in other ways.

Creating a Challenge

Objective.   To make learning enjoyable and profitable.

Explanation.   When learning occurs because of student effort, we call that challenge. When a student need not make an effort, we call that boredom. When a student makes an effort and fails, we call that frustration. A challenging learning climate is the desirable one.

Suggestions

1. Try to set goals for each lesson that you believe are within the grasp of your students if they make an effort.
2. When you notice that your students can succeed without effort and that their attention seems to drift away, change the activity or step up the tempo.
3. When you notice that your students are weary and unsuccessful, change the activity or slow the tempo.

4. When you begin a new type of activity, make it last only a short period. For example, tell your students that you will be working with them on an activity for ten minutes. At the end of that time determine if they want to do more or want a change.
5. Make certain that your students know when they have been successful. Illustrate their successes in a variety of ways. Have them self-evaluate. If they do not believe they have done well when they have, then discuss the goals and the resulting behaviors that were successful.

Encouraging Risk-Taking

Objective.   To encourage your students to try, even when things appear to be difficult.

Explanation.   Learning involves a certain amount of risk-taking. If people try and are wrong, then learning can become very unpleasant. If people do not try, then they cannot be wrong, but they won't learn either. Tutors can make adjustments that will enhance risk-taking.

Suggestions.   Many of the suggestions presented in this chapter encourage risk-taking. Focusing on strengths, asking personal questions, and attending to student interests are just a few of the ideas that are discussed.
    Here are a few additional suggestions:

1. Plan seating arrangements that make it seem you are a helper instead of a threat. Sitting beside a student instead of across a desk is one helpful seating adjustment.
2. Encourage students to work in pairs when it is appropriate. Pairing encourages risk-taking because the students work out their responses before sharing them with the teacher or tutor. For example, students can work together making reports, checking their arithmetic, or preparing oral reading.
3. Plan a system for communicating with your students. You

might develop a place where notes can be dropped off and picked up. Helping students evaluate their performance (described under "Helping Students Pay Attention") also enhances communication.

Using Questioning Strategies

Objective.   To help students respond during questioning.

Explanation.   Sometimes students are afraid to respond to questions. They may have been embarrassed in the past when they came up with incorrect answers. Tutors must make plans for questioning that will encourage students to respond fully, without fear of embarrassment. The following suggestions show ways tutors can use questioning effectively.

Suggestions
1.   Allow time for students to prepare answers. Tutors sometimes expect immediate responses and interrupt the thought process with more questions.
2.   Prepare questions that are personal. Personal questions are those that have no "right" answers. For example:
     • What did you like best about that story?
     • What part of the story was most interesting to you?
     • Tell me what you think was the most important event in that story.
3.   Create a discussion atmosphere. Instead of a series of unrelated questions, share your feelings about the story. The purpose of questioning is to develop a thorough understanding of what has been read. Have your students develop their own questions to ask you. Being able to create a question requires careful thought.
4.   Prepare questions that encourage thinking. Many tutors fall into the trap of asking questions that require students to recall facts. For example: "Who was the other girl in this story?" "What was the dog's name?" Instead, ask questions that let students think carefully about the story and require more than a one-word answer. For example: "Why do you

think Margi liked her dog so much?" "Who did you think did the right thing with his dog?" "Why?"

5. Allow for different ways of answering questions. Some students would rather reply orally, while others might prefer to write their answers. Some students like to answer into a tape recorder. Search for ways to make your students comfortable when responding to questions.

Developing a Comfortable Learning Environment

Objective.   To place the student in a comfortable learning situation.

Explanation.   Learning can be enhanced when the environment is comfortable. If it is too hot, too cold, or too stuffy, then it is difficult for students to enjoy the learning activity. This is true even when the activity is well-planned and interesting. Tutors do not always have control over all features of the learning environment, but they should attempt to make adjustments when they are needed.

Suggestions
1. Do little things to make the area pleasant. A poster or some pictures can help to make a drab area inviting. A smiley face on the chalkboard can be effective.
2. Pay attention to the temperature. If you are in a room that is too hot or too cold, try to make a change. If you cannot, adapt to the situation. When it is too cold, be certain to plan some physical activities between parts of your session. If it is too hot, try to keep physical activities to a minimum.
3. Try to be sure that your area has good ventilation. Open a window, or get near a door or ventilation fan. If you cannot do this, ask your contact person for help.
4. Watch out for distracting noise. If you are next door to the music room, gymnasium, or other noise-producing places, learning might be very difficult. Ask for a different area for tutoring if noise becomes a problem.

An important tutoring strategy is to place the student in a comfortable learning situation.

5.   Be sure that chairs and desks are the appropriate size for your students. If they are not, ask for them to be changed.

6.   Try to make the area personally meaningful for your students. Perhaps you can have some of their past good work available for them to see. A personal photograph or artwork might have appeal for some students.

TEACHING PLANS FOR SPECIFIC TUTORING STRATEGIES

Reading Books to Students

Objective. To stimulate interest in literature and reading by reading aloud to students.

Procedures
1. Briefly discuss the value of reading aloud to students including such ideas as:
   • Reading to students exposes them to types of literature they might like but would not have selected themselves.
   • Oral reading can bring another more vivid dimension to a story.
   • The enjoyment of hearing stories may motivate students to read more on their own.
2. Provide specific examples that delineate different facets of sharing books:
   • *Book Selection.* Ask tutors to consider their students' interests and attention span in the selection of books. Discuss the value of letting the student choose the book to be read during the session.
   • *Introducing the Book.* Suggest a few ways to introduce a book meaningfully. You might talk about some interesting aspect of the book or ask a question about the title or a picture.
   • *Reading the Book.* Discuss how to encourage interest in the story by using expression when reading and involving the student at appropriate moments.
   • *Reflecting on the Story.* Suggest ways to encourage discussion of the story after it is read. Some students enjoy discussing a favorite incident or character while others may like a questioning game (see Appendix D for specific examples).

Resource Material
Larrick, Nancy. *A Parent's Guide to Children's Reading.* New York: Bantam Books, 1975.

Developing Comprehension Through Discussion

Objective.   To encourage students to discuss ideas gained from a passage without fear of being wrong (an alternative to questioning).

Procedures
1.   Discuss the importance of letting students react to the material they read in an atmosphere of acceptance.
2.   Provide specific examples:
    a. The tutor and student can discuss topics related to the reading material such as:
        • the pros and cons of issues in the passage
        • what they believe to be characters' motives for certain acts
        • the importance of certain critical events in the passage
        • ways of changing the ending of the story
        • why they think the author wrote the story
        If the tutor is working with a small group, a student monitor can be designated to lead it. That person is responsible for keeping the discussion on the selected topic. Tutors might want to model the monitor role several times so that students understand the responsibilities.
    b. Discuss with tutors their role of authority. Explain that their ideas and opinions are not to be forced upon the students. Their responses to their students' ideas can affect enthusiasm and interest. Such responses as: "Really, I hadn't thought of that," "Let's talk about that some more," and "Of course, good thinking" are likely to generate continued student discussion. Likewise, responses such as: "Read it again, that's not the point being made," "Really?" and "Don't you think . . ." tend to stifle discussion.
        Remind tutors that the purpose of a discussion mode is to generate student language about the passage just read. If this is to occur, the student must feel that responses are not criticized.

Resource Material

Pearson, P. David, and Johnson, Dale D. *Teaching Reading Comprehension*. New York: Holt, Rinehart and Winston, 1978.

Rowe, Mary Budd. *Teaching Science as Continuous Inquiry*. New York: McGraw-Hill, 1973.

Developing Personal Outlines

Objective. To enable students to reorganize the authors' ideas into personally meaningful outlines.

Procedures
1. Start with a personal question, for example:
   • What do you think was important in that story?
   • What one idea do you think is worth remembering?
   • What interested you most about this story?

   With such questions the student has an answer that is personally meaningful. That answer does not need to match what the teacher is thinking.
2. Answers are recorded on paper or the chalkboard. Tutors do not indicate approval ("Right, Wrong"). They accept the responses and show their acceptance by writing down all answers for future discussion.
3. After several responses have been recorded, students select the one of their choice and go back to the story to find statements that support the idea selected. These supporting ideas are placed into a personal outline format:

      1. _____

                    important idea

        a. _____

                    supporting detail

        b. _____

                    supporting detail

4. Once the personal outline is completed, tutors can discuss the appropriateness of the idea selected and the supporting details. At times we recommend going back to the pages

where the selected idea is found and working together to select appropriate ideas and details.

The technique of developing personal outlines has special impact for reading material in content areas such as science and social studies.

Resource Material
Wilson, Robert M., et al. *Programmed Reading.* Columbus, Ohio: Merrill, 1980.

Figuring Out Unfamiliar Words

Objective.   To provide students with a variety of questions they can ask when faced with an unfamiliar word. These questions will help them figure out the meaning and pronunciation of these words.

Procedures
1. Explain that difficult words can cause students to become confused and stop reading. They need a strategy to use when faced with an unfamiliar word.
2. Provide specific examples:
    a. Give tutors a word in a sentence, such as, "The woman gave the sick child some *medicine.*" Ask them how they would figure out the word if they didn't know it.
    b. Note the importance of using clues in the sentence. Tell tutors that a *first* strategy students can use for figuring out unknown words is to read to the end of the sentence for meaning clues. Students can ask themselves:
        • What word would make sense in this sentence? Why? What clues can be found in the other parts of the sentence or in the sentences nearby?
        Discuss other strategies to use in conjunction with the clues that can be found in the sentence. Encourage tutors to have their students ask the following additional questions:
        • Does the beginning part of the word look like the

beginning part of another word that I do know? Does this word fit into the sentence?
- Do I recognize any other parts of the word, such as the middle or the end? Does the word that is suggested fit in the sentence?
- Can I sound out the word? Does the word I just pronounced fit into the sentence?
- How else can I find out the meaning of the word? (Ask a friend, or consult the glossary or a dictionary.)

Resource Material

Johnson, Dale, and Pearson, P. David. *Teaching Reading Vocabulary.* New York: Holt, Rinehart & Winston, 1978.

Ways to Learn New Vocabulary

Objective.   To help students learn the meaning and pronunciation of new words.

Procedures
1.   Explain the need for students to repeatedly practice words so they will recognize these words quickly rather than having to sound them out.
2.   Provide specific examples:
  a. Discuss the procedures for developing word cards. Explain that words for study can come from any reading material (newspapers, magazines, textbooks). Allow tutors to make a word card on a three-by-five card, putting the word on the front and composing a sentence on the back. Example:
  - motorcycle (on front of card). I want a blue and black *motorcycle* (on back of card).

     Discuss the importance of allowing students to select the word to be studied, compose the sentence, and underline the word once it is written in a sentence.
  b. Discuss the variety of activities that can be done with the word cards so the students will have repeated practice using them. Examples:

- Have students go through their word cards to find words that name things, show action, or describe things.
- Take turns with students making up meaning clues about the words on the cards. (A first clue for *motorcycle* might be "a machine with two wheels that moves very fast.")
- Make a game that can be played with the word cards, such as word bingo or lotto. (See "Playing Educational Games to Increase Vocabulary" below for a complete example.)

Resource Material
Johnson, Dale, and Pearson, P. David. *Teaching Reading Vocabulary.* New York: Holt, Rinehart & Winston, 1978.

Playing Educational Games to Increase Vocabulary

Objective.   To help students learn new words through the use of games.

Procedures
1. Briefly explain why the game format is being used, noting that games can be enjoyable learning tools.
2. Provide specific examples:
   a. Discuss how tutors can make simple game boards that are geared directly to the students' interests by using themes of sports, animals, and cars. Show examples of these types of games. (See Appendix B for suggestions.)
   b. Explain how words are to be selected for the games. The students' teachers and the students themselves are the best sources for this. The importance of presenting words in a sentence as an aid to meaning might also be highlighted.
   c. Give the tutors an opportunity to make games.
   d. Suggestions for game-playing are important. Tips on ways to respond to right and wrong answers, ways to give

Helping students increase vocabulary through games is a useful tutoring strategy.

hints, and methods to allow the students to legitimately win might be included. (See Appendix C for further suggestions.)

Resource Material
Sullivan, D.; Davey, H. B.; and Dickerson, D. *Games as Learning Tools.*
     Paoli, Pa.: Instructo, 1978.

Rereading Strategies

Objective.   To enhance comprehension and develop fluency by helping students achieve automatic word recognition skills.
     To encourage students to shift their focus from individual words to the use of meaning and sentence structure clues.

Procedures
1.   Stress the importance of giving students repeated practice with words so they will know them immediately upon seeing

them. Discuss the value of reading sentences rather than just lists of isolated words.

2.   Provide specific examples:

a. Give tutors a short paragraph and ask them to read it aloud at least twice to the person next to them. Discuss the difference between the first and second readings, noting the benefits students who are experiencing difficulty in reading might receive from this activity.

b. Discuss activities they could use to give students practice with rereading.

The following suggestions can be used:

• Select high interest material that students can successfully read.

Repeated reading (to be done with one student at a time)

• Ask students to read a short passage of approximately seventy-five words silently.

• Have students read to you, and record the reading rate. (If students make more than five mispronunciations per hundred words, this passage is too difficult and another should be selected.)

• Have students read the passage aloud again, and chart the reading rate. (The second reading is generally much smoother than the first.)

• Allow students to read the passage at least three times and show them how both rate and fluency have increased.

Echo reading (to be done with one student at a time)

• Tell students to read aloud with you while running their eyes smoothly across the page.

• Sit next to students and hold the reading material with them.

• Begin reading with students, allowing your voice to be slightly louder and faster. As you read, move your finger along with the line of print.

• Passages should be read a number of times so fluency will be achieved.

• As students become more confident in reading, soften

your voice and let theirs be the loudest. Students may also want to take your role of running a finger under the print as you read.

Resource material

Samuels, S. Jay. "The Method of Repeated Readings." *Reading Teacher,* 32 (January 1979): 403–08.

Tierney, Robert J.; Readence, John E.; and Dishner, Ernest K. *Reading Strategies and Practices: A Guide for Improving Instruction.* Boston: Allyn and Bacon, 1980. Pp. 139–41.

Using Students' Stories as Reading Material

Objective. To develop comprehension and vocabulary skills and increase confidence in reading by using student-produced material.

Procedures

1. Briefly discuss the benefits of using students' own writing as material for teaching beginning and remedial readers. Include ideas such as:
    a. The language in student-dictated material is familiar to them because it is similar to their own speech.
    b. Students understand the ideas in the stories and are generally interested in them since they themselves produced them.
2. Provide specific examples:
    a. Demonstrate to the tutors the procedures used in getting a student to dictate a story.
    b. Have tutors practice getting a student to dictate a story by role-playing the student/tutor situation. Have one play the tutor and one the student. The following plan can be used:
        Story dictation:
        (1) Talk with students about something in which you know they are interested.
             Example: a sports event or a television program. (When you have time to prepare in advance, you

can bring in something to make or discuss.) After discussing the topic, tell students you are going to write down their words so you both will have a story (or directions, a recipe, or a description).

(2)   Record the exact words and word order that the students employ. Use correct spelling, write clearly, and sit so they can read the words you are writing.

(3)   Read the story with the students.

Answer the tutors' questions about this dictation procedure, analyzing the importance of writing the students' *exact* words even if they are not grammatically correct.

c. Discuss ways to build vocabulary and comprehension skills with student stories. The following are a few activities that help students focus on the ideas and words in their stories.

(1)   Ask them to select words from the story that they know at the moment but would like to learn so as to know them in other stories.

(2)   Write each word on a three-by-five card. Ask students to use the word in a sentence and record it on the back of the word card. Let the students read the sentence and underline the new word. Save these word cards so they can be used in other activities. (See "Ways to Learn New Vocabulary" on page 69 for specific examples.)

(3)   Cross out every tenth word in the story and ask students to figure out the missing word. (This activity focuses on use of context clues.)

(4)   Take turns making up and asking each other questions about the story. When possible, locate the specific words or phrases that answer each question. Questions might deal with the following types of information:

• What happened?

• How and why did it happen?

• What would you have done if . . . ?

(This activity focuses on understanding parts of the story.)

(5)   Take turns writing the types of questions discussed in the preceding activity. (This activity focuses on understanding parts of the story and encourages the writing of ideas.)

Resource Material

Hall, M. A. *Teaching Reading as a Language Experience.* Columbus, Ohio: Merrill, 1976.

Stauffer, Russell G. *The Language Experience Approach to the Teaching of Reading.* New York: Harper & Row, 1980.

Using Functional Materials

Objective.   To develop school-type skills using materials from outside the school as a base for instruction.

Procedures

1.   Stress the need for students to be aware that what they are learning in school can be applied to materials outside the school. Indicate the survival nature of such instruction.
2.   Provide specific examples:
    a.   Conduct a workshop on how to use the newspaper to teach reading and arithmetic skills. Show how consumer awareness can be developed using newspapers. Show how figurative language is used on the sports page and how cause-and-effect relationships are in almost every news article.
    b.   Conduct similar workshops using magazines, telephone books, labels from food boxes and medicine bottles, and other outside materials. When conducting the workshops, have the tutors do the activities that they will be asking their students to perform.
    c.   Show tutors how to make learning centers and games using these materials. Actually construct the games and centers in the workshop.
    d.   Have tutors bring outside materials to school so that ways can be designed for them to use the materials in instruction.

Resource Material

Hartshorn, Merrill F., ed. *ANPA Foundation Bibliography: Newspaper in Education Publications.* 2d ed. Washington, D.C.: American Newspaper Publishers Association, 1978.

Sullivan, Dorothy; Davey, H. Beth; and Dickerson, Dolores. *Games as Learning Tools.* Paoli, Pa.: Instructo, 1977.

Wilson, Robert M., and Barnes, Marcia M. *Survival Learning Materials.* York, Pa.: College Reading Association, 1974.

TEACHING PLAN FOR COMMON TUTOR PROBLEMS

Objective.   To prepare tutors for some difficulties that may arise as they work with students.

Procedures

1.   Tell tutors that there are common problems that they may encounter.
2.   Provide specific examples:

    Identify some of the common problems and work out alternative solutions as a group. The following list contains a few questions frequently asked by tutors. Some suggestions for dealing with these problems are also given.

- What do I do if a student does not want to try an activity?
  Suggestions:
  —Tell the student you know that it is difficult, but that you are there to help.
  —Urge the student to try, and explain that a mistake will not be counted against him or her.
  —Do the first part of the activity together as a team. Then let the student try it alone.
- What do I do if the student is bored?
  Suggestions:
  —Reexamine the activity to make certain it is appropriate.
  —Move the student into a decision-making role—for example, given three activities, which one would he or she prefer?
  —Check to see if the student might be missing an exciting

activity in the classroom. If so, suggest that the two of you return to participate.

- What do I do if a student fails to bring necessary materials to the tutoring session?
Suggestions:
—Have extra materials available.
—Make a plan so that this is less likely to happen again. Try checking with the student before leaving the pick-up area to make sure everything that is needed is on hand, or write a note together to remind the student to bring things for the next session.
- What do I do if a student breaks school rules?
Suggestions:
—Go over school rules to be certain that the student knows them.
—Try to determine why the student broke the rules. Were there circumstances that would explain the behavior?
—Seek the advice of the tutoring coordinator.
- What do I do if a student seems angry or upset a lot?
Suggestions:

If you have not been able to find out what the problem is by talking with the student, you might try the following ideas:
—Be at the place of tutoring before the student so you can greet him or her and start immediately with a high interest activity. Some students have trouble with transitions and may become upset when working with a new person in a different setting. Help the student feel at ease and cared for as quickly as possible.
—Develop activities that are fun and that frequently make the student feel successful. Your student may have been failing in the classroom. This student may be afraid, angry, and embarrassed because another person is going to find out that he or she is a failure.
—Talk with the student's teacher about the specific behavior of the student. Ask how the student feels about going to tutoring, whether a favorite activity is being

missed, or if the work load is overwhelming. The teacher will be able to give you some guidance for working with this student.

• What do I do if a student doesn't understand an activity?
  Suggestions:
  —Break the activity into small parts and let the student work on one part at a time.
  —Explain the activity using easier words and examples related to the student's life. Use pictures or concrete objects when appropriate.
  —Do the activity with the student, explaining each step as you progress. Let the student do the first part with you. Gradually let him or her do new steps independently while you complete and explain those that have not yet been mastered. Do this until the whole activity can be performed independently. At this point be sure you are available to give encouragement.

• What do I do if a student gives incorrect answers and I want to focus on student strengths?
  Suggestions:
  —Compliment good thinking and urge the student to focus on another possible solution.
  —Look for parts of the response that were correct.
  —Provide time for the student to rethink the response without any reaction from you.

8 Teacher Participation

ORGANIZER

This chapter focuses on the background information teachers need for full participation in the tutoring program. Suggestions for teacher orientation are given for four areas.

If you are interested in:

- tutor-training, see page 80.
- administrative procedures, see page 81.
- teacher-tutor relationships, see page 81.
- encouraging student participation, see page 82.

TEACHERS need to understand the details of a new program so they can take full advantage of its benefits. Those who are going to have students in a tutoring program usually have many questions about procedures and can be a tremendous help to the tutors and students if they are well-informed. It is helpful to provide teachers with background information before the program actually begins. At first teachers are most concerned with details relating to (1) tutor-training, (2) administrative procedures involving schedulings, (3) teacher-tutor relationships, and (4) encouraging student participation. The following are a few suggestions for discussing these areas with teachers. (Teachers may also enjoy reading a few articles about tutoring; selected references can be found on pages 123–25.)

TUTOR-TRAINING

Teachers are particularly interested in the skills tutors bring. If given a packet of tutor-training materials and guided briefly through the types of activities in which tutors will participate, teachers will more clearly understand tutor-training. Since these initial tutor-training sessions are not the only source of training the tutors will receive, the teachers' role in future training should be discussed. If the coordinator continues to provide guidance after the early training, day-to-day supervision of tutors is not a major concern of the teachers. Each teacher, however, will need to provide time for occasional conferences with tutors. These may be brief biweekly or monthly meetings where the teacher gives praise and suggestions, and the tutors have an opportunity to ask questions. If, however, the teacher is completely in charge of the tutors, then they need to meet often (possibly weekly at first) and regularly. As with any new program, concerns usually decrease as tutors become familiar with the students and the procedures.

80

ADMINISTRATIVE PROCEDURES

While the coordinator is usually most helpful to tutors in regard to settling them into their routine, teachers can also be of assistance if they are given the same information the tutors have. Materials such as the tutoring schedule, procedures for getting materials, and information about where questions can be answered all help teachers understand the scope and procedures of the program. Of special concern to teachers are the procedures for dealing with student absence. Teachers need to notify tutors in advance when their students have other plans (such as an assembly or class trip). If teachers can regularly make sure tutors are informed about planned absences, they can avoid having tutors feel that their time and work are not valued.

TEACHER-TUTOR RELATIONSHIPS

Teachers sometimes don't realize how much their words of encouragement and appreciation mean to tutors. Whenever possible, the tutors need to know their work is important. The initial conference is a wonderful time for tutors to find out specifically what they have done well, be encouraged, and ask questions. The tutor information form (figure 5) will help the teacher know the tutor better and make suggestions with his or her specific skills in mind.

Since some tutors may be a little ill at ease when they begin, teachers generally need to set a date (early in the tutoring program) for an initial conference. Teachers may also want to encourage future meetings. It is also helpful to suggest times of the day when it is convenient for a casual question to be asked. This lets the tutors know that it is all right to ask short questions and protects the teachers from being interrupted at inconvenient times.

Even though some teachers and tutors may not meet often formally, their relationship can be continued when passing in the hall, or in the minute when the student is picked up or dropped off. This is a time when a greeting, a smile, and a comment about something the student has enjoyed with the tutor is appreciated. A short list of guidelines, as those shown in figure 18, can be given to teachers to remind them of successful ways of working with tutors.

ENCOURAGING STUDENT PARTICIPATION

Students are generally enthusiastic about tutoring and eagerly await the tutor's arrival. Some, however, may feel uncomfortable about being away from their classes, while others may have problems, such as not remembering the time of tutoring. With just a little planning, teachers can easily help these students. Teachers can play a major role in initiating and sustaining student interest by showing that they value tutoring. This can be done in the following ways:

1. Anticipate with students the enjoyable things to be done in tutoring.
2. Help students establish a routine associated with tutoring, such as putting away books or watching the clock for the appropriate time. Sometimes setting a paper clock with the time the student is to leave the classroom is helpful.
3. Make sure students are *not* required to make up all the classwork missed during the tutoring time. Going to

FIGURE 18   Guidelines for Teachers Working with Tutors

- Greet tutors with a smile and a comment about something their students have enjoyed doing with them.

- Let tutors know their work is important by:
  —utilizing their skills effectively
  —notifying them of a schedule change as soon as you are aware of it

- Provide a convenient time for them to ask you questions and get assistance.

- Feel free to discuss problems or suggestions with your tutoring program coordinators.

---

tutoring gets to be a punishment if students have to do both activities.

4. Ask students about their tutoring activities and encourage them to share with the class particularly interesting things they have done during tutoring sessions.

9 Sustaining the Tutoring Program

ORGANIZER

This chapter focuses on ways to keep the participants in the tutoring program enthusiastic and on strategies for evaluating the program.
    If you are interested in:

- ideas for supporting the tutor, see page 86.
- ideas for supporting the teacher, see page 90.
- ideas for supporting the students, see page 91.
- suggestions related to evaluation, see page 92.

NOW that the program is in operation, don't stop giving it your creative energy and attention. A program needs continuous tender loving care to maintain the initial enthusiasm of the participants and to avoid high tutor turnover and teacher disenchantment. Everyone needs to work together to give support to the tutors, teachers, and students, and the program must be evaluated on a regular basis.

SUPPORTING THE TUTOR

Showing Appreciation

Everyone wants to be appreciated, and so do the tutors. They work with students conscientiously and need to be treated with respect and to know their work is valued. The following areas are just a few ways to give tutors the recognition they deserve.

1. Put up a bulletin board with pictures of the tutors, create attractive ID buttons, and have notes placed in the school bulletin about tutoring activities. These activities both tell the tutors they are important and also help others in the school become acquainted with them (see figure 19).
2. Encourage school staff members to greet the tutors and help them feel comfortable in their new positions. (Teachers should be provided with a list of tutor names.)
3. Provide ways to recognize the tutors' contributions formally. In addition to telling tutors the good things they are doing and thanking them for the work they have done, teachers and coordinators often plan an end-of-the year party and/or give an award (figure 20) noting specific activities in which tutors participated. Teachers may also help students make or write something special for their tutors, who greatly value these ways of showing appreciation.

FIGURE 19   Examples of Appreciation

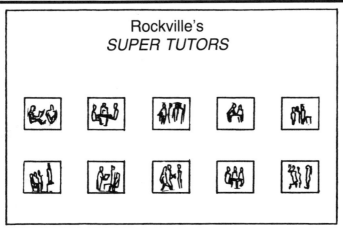

Bulletin Board of School Tutors

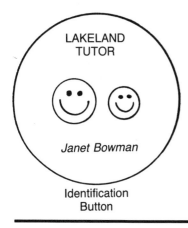

Identification
Button

SCHOOL NEWS
BULLETIN

We ate well!
Karen Johnson and Todd
Thompson were sharing their
delicious peanut butter candy
with friends of the Kent tutoring
program. We can't wait for next
week's treat. See Todd or
Karen if you have a sweet tooth
and want a quick "no-bake"
recipe.

Providing In-service Training

Initial training helps the tutors get started, but as they become
familiar with their situations, they generally develop many new
questions about teaching. Weekly or biweekly group meetings
give the tutors an opportunity to share their successes and problems and to obtain new ideas. The topics of these regular meetings can change as the needs and interests of the tutors develop.
While the coordinator may conduct these sessions, other
teachers can serve as resources. An example of a typical plan for

FIGURE 20   Tutor Award

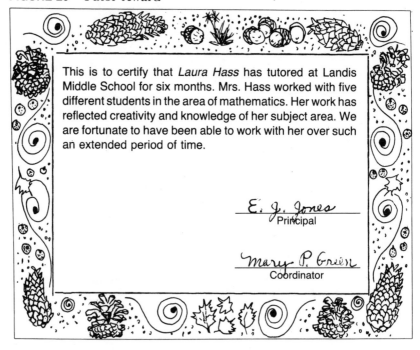

This is to certify that *Laura Hass* has tutored at Landis Middle School for six months. Mrs. Hass worked with five different students in the area of mathematics. Her work has reflected creativity and knowledge of her subject area. We are fortunate to have been able to work with her over such an extended period of time.

E. J. Jones
Principal

Mary P. Green
Coordinator

a tutor meeting is shown in figure 21. Tutors may also need to meet individually with the teacher or coordinator to get information about their teaching and to have an opportunity to ask specific questions about their students.

FIGURE 21   Weekly Meetings With Tutors

Fourth Weekly Meeting

School   Brown High School

Date   March 6

Time: thirty minutes

Please include the following topics in your discussion with tutors:

Successful Tutoring Experiences

Share with tutors things you have observed them doing that were particularly successful or interesting.

FIGURE 21   (continued)

Examples:

Games.   Mention games tutors have made that are colorful, clear, and well-constructed, have a new twist to them (an artistic or interesting marker or new scoring), or are products of their own imagination. Have tutors share the games you mention and add their own comments.

Books.   Tell tutors you have seen their students absorbed and very interested in the reading of library books. Ask them what things they do to keep their students interested in their books.
Suggestions: (1) picking books that contain topics of interest to the students; (2) reading to the students with expression; (3) asking students to listen to the story to find out the answer to a particular question; (4) taking turns reading with students; and (5) letting students read when the tutor knows they will be successful.

Problems Related to Tutoring

Ask tutors if they have had any problems. Let other tutors help solve the problems.

Evaluation of Tutoring

Comment on interesting remarks tutors have made in their logs and encourage tutors to keep making notes. (Some teachers have had the tutors get together in pairs and discuss each other's comments. Teachers of school-age tutors have collected tutors' logs for a day so they could read them.)

Participation in Tutoring

Encourage tutors to begin and end tutoring approximately within twenty minutes. *Reinforce the necessity for marking the attendance sheet.* When working with young tutors, you might choose one tutor to alert others to begin and end tutoring and to remind them to check the attendance sheet.

New Game Ideas

Have tutors share any new games they have tried or made. Discuss need to play a *variety* of games. Some teachers have strongly suggested that tutors should make or use at least one new game weekly. Give new game ideas for their booklets and explain, play, and/or make the games.

Checking Administrative Procedures

The coordinator needs to check initial tutoring procedures to see if they are being followed. A few questions that can be asked to get at particular concerns of tutors are:

1. Are you being notified when your students are not going to be available for tutoring?
2. Do you feel comfortable in the place where you are tutoring?
3. Are instructional materials easily accessible?
4. Have you had difficulty solving problems you've encountered in tutoring?

SUPPORTING THE TEACHER

If teachers can voice their concerns and know that these will be heard and dealt with, they are generally eager to participate in a tutoring program. If time is provided for sharing problems in an atmosphere of acceptance and mutual respect, constructive suggestions from both experienced and inexperienced teachers usually result. The coordinator may find that monthly group meetings and frequent individual conferences are sufficient to get a sense of how teachers feel about tutoring and to deal with their concerns.

In addition to being able to discuss their perceptions of the program, teachers, like every member of the educational community, need recognition for their participation. Tutors can be encouraged to show their appreciation by acknowledging the considerate things teachers do for them and by commenting on the interesting things they observe teachers doing in the classroom. As well as giving the teacher supportive comments, the principal or coordinator can also write a letter of appreciation for their support. The coordinator of a tutoring program should be sure to include participating teachers in special tutoring events, such as a luncheon or a tea, as a way of thanking them for the many extra hours spent on behalf of their students. Original awards and other activities like small skits have added an extra personal touch to such occasions.

SUPPORTING THE STUDENT

The students are the ones who ultimately need to be contented and feel comfortable with the program. If there are student concerns about tutoring, the following questions may determine factors that are contributing to the problem:

1. Is the content of tutoring meaningful and appropriate?
2. Is the teacher interested in the tutoring activities?
3. Is the student required to do all the classwork that is missed because of participation in tutoring?
4. Are the parents supporting the child's participation in tutoring?

Students also enjoy being recognized for their involvement in tutoring. To give a feeling of group accomplishment, tutors have planned special activities such as picnics, treasure hunts, and pizza parties as an enjoyable way to end a tutoring program. Participation awards such as the one in figure 22 have also been highly valued by the students.

FIGURE 22   Student Award

SOMETHING TO "ROAR" ABOUT!

GREAT JOB AWARD
for

Cheryl Kennedy

EVALUATING THE TUTORING PROGRAM

One factor that distinguishes between successful and unsuccessful tutoring programs is their flexibility. Successful programs adapt to meet the needs of the school. Coordinators of these programs continually evaluate their procedures to fit the changing needs of tutors and students. They find that discussions and careful observation are effective ways to gather information. Informal conversations with teachers and tutors and frequent observation of the actual tutoring process are excellent strategies for learning about the program. Meetings with tutors and teachers provide an additional way to learn what is going well and what concerns people have. Because tutors will come in contact with many people in the school, those other staff members need to be asked for their suggestions. The media specialists, secretaries, lunchroom workers, custodians, and special teachers all may have ways to improve the program.

In addition to these informal assessments, written evaluation forms can be given to all members of the school community ranging from parents to principal. Some people feel more comfortable expressing themselves in writing than in a group meeting or individual conference. Often a program's positive aspects, as well as problems, are described in more detail on a written form. Written evaluations also provide tangible documentation of a program's success and can be used as evidence supporting its continuation. Examples of a few types of evaluation forms are shown in figures 23, 24, and 25. If reactions are gathered from parents, teachers, tutors, students, and any other people involved with tutoring, the program will be better able to develop an atmosphere conducive to student growth and development.

At times it will be useful to observe tutors formally to obtain evaluation information. The tutor coordinator might observe prior to a weekly tutor-training session to determine areas that need attention. A teacher might want to observe a tutor's use of a particular teaching strategy. Information from one of the evaluation forms might alert school personnel to some unusual (good or bad) tutoring activities.

When observations are being made, the purposes of the tutoring need to be considered. There are some general items,

FIGURE 23 Questionnaire for Teachers

Teacher's name

Grade

		Very Negative		Neutral		Very Positive
1.	Your students' reaction to their participation in the tutoring program.	1	2	3	4	5

How many students from your class would you want to participate:

_____All   _____%   _____None

2.	Your reaction to having your students participate in a tutoring program.	1	2	3	4	5

3. How often during the week should tutoring sessions be held?

_____

4. How long should each tutoring session be? _____

5. *Comments and Suggestions*

_____

_____

_____

_____

_____

_____

---

however, that could be on any observation checklist. They include:

1. Is the tutor arriving at the scheduled time?
2. Is the tutor making the student feel good about the session?

FIGURE 24   Questionnaire for Tutors

Tutor's name

Please circle your answers for questions 1 through 4

1. Would you like to be a tutor again?   NO   YES

2. Do you think your student improved
    in ___[subject of tutoring]___ ?   NO   YES

3. Do you think your student enjoyed
    coming to the tutoring session?   NO   Sometimes   YES

4. Do you like the weekly meetings
    with the other tutors?   NO   Sometimes   YES

    Why or why not? _____

    _____

5. *Comments and Suggestions*

    _____

    _____

    _____

    _____

    _____

    _____

3.   Does the tutor come to the session prepared with neces-
     sary instructional materials?
4.   Does the session appear to be well-planned?
5.   Are instructional strategies appropriate?

If the answer to a question on a checklist is "yes," then a check can be placed opposite the item. If the answer is "no" or "unclear," comments should be made so that corrective action can be taken. The observation is not intended to rate the tutor or to compare one tutor with another. Therefore negative com-

FIGURE 25   Questionnaire for Students

	Student's name		

Please answer these questions:

1. Do you like working with your tutor?   YES   Sometimes   NO

2. Do you want to keep on working
   with your tutor?   YES   NO

3. Do you want to have a new
   tutor?   YES   NO

4. Do you think tutoring has helped
   you learn more?   YES   NO

5. What do you like about tutoring?

   _____

   _____

   _____

6. What don't you like about tutoring?

   _____

   _____

   _____

ments should be avoided, and all suggestions should be constructive in nature.

Tutors should receive feedback as soon as possible after an observation. It is especially effective to spend a few minutes immediately following the tutoring session.

10 Additional Thoughts on Tutoring

ORGANIZER

This chapter focuses on a few additional topics you should consider when developing a tutoring program.

If you are interested in:

- special tutoring situations, see page 98.
- financial considerations, see page 102.
- legal considerations, see page 102.
- a tutoring checklist, see page 103.

SEVERAL aspects of tutoring programs remain to be dealt with. A few cautions about special tutoring situations, discussion of financial and legal matters, and the inclusion of a checklist make up this chapter.

SPECIAL TUTORING SITUATIONS

Some situations require special skills and knowledge on the part of tutors. Tutor-training sessions will need to address these situations directly to help the tutors avoid serious problems. Four such special situations are suggested in this chapter. Each school will be able to identify others that are peculiar to the school setting. The four discussed here are: (1) tutoring students with disabilities, (2) tutors working with their own children at home, (3) tutoring more than one student, and (4) team tutoring.

Tutoring Students with Disabilities. Tutors need to be aware of the current views on the teaching of children with disabilities. Disabled students are likely candidates for tutoring, and tutors can play a vital role in their education. Some of the following views will serve as a base of information about working with these students:

1. Persons with disabilities are handicapped when the situation in which they must learn has not been or cannot be adjusted to their disabilities. If the system can adjust to a disability, then the person is not handicapped in that situation. For example, a ramp makes access to buildings possible for those confined to wheelchairs.
2. Under the law students with disabilities are to learn in regular classrooms whenever feasible. In this way disabled students can feel as normal as possible, and non-disabled students can realize the disabled are normal.
3. Since many teachers cannot provide the time and attention to work with disabled students, these children can

become frustrated. A tutor might be able to provide that
time and attention.

4.   The resources of the school should be available to tutors
     who agree to work with the disabled. Special education
     teachers, reading teachers, classroom teachers, school
     nurses, librarians, and administrators all might have
     some special help to offer.

Disabled students are also required by law to be provided
with an Individualized Eduation Program (IEP). It is not likely
that tutors would be written into an IEP. However, if they are
working with these students, they should know the nature and
goals of the IEP. They need to understand the role of parental
approval in the IEP and the nature of the evaluation that will
take place.

Tutors Working with Their Own Children at Home.   Many tutors
use their training to instruct their own children in the home.
While such activities are not a part of tutor program objectives,
our experience is that they do take place and need special attention.

Regardless of their effectiveness in the schools, tutors are not
always the best people to be working with their own children. We
can all relate to the stories of parents who cannot teach their own
children to drive an automobile and yet can teach a neighbor's
son or daughter. The concern for success, the need to see one's
own child as the best, and the pressure that such tutoring can
place upon the child are but a few of the problems.

Parents are often in a situation, however, when tutoring
their own children is necessary and advantageous. Parents, after
all, were primarily responsible for teaching their children prior
to school entry. When the child comes home from school with a
difficult assignment, what is the parent to do but pitch in? And
when the child is frustrated and disappointed with a learning
activity at home, it seems sensible and desirable for the parents to
help out. Since most parents will be working with their children
whether the school recommends it or not, the school should
assist them to be as effective as possible. If the parent is a tutor in
the school, then it seems all the more desirable that the school

help assure an effective parent-child learning relationship. Each case is different, but a few guidelines might be suggested for parent tutors to consider.

1. Keep the tutoring situation pleasant. When things become unpleasant, it is time to stop or change the activity.
2. Plan for short periods of work. Determine the amount of time needed and let the child help establish a time frame. Otherwise the child might begin to feel as though the session is never-ending. Ten to fifteen minutes is the recommended maximum time for young children.
3. Whenever possible, place the child in a decision-making situation. Children can make decisions about (a) how much time is needed, (b) when and where to work, (c) how much help they need, and many other things.
4. Focus on strengths. Parents should consistently focus upon their children's successes. All parents should know that their children want to be successful in their parents' eyes. Parents should be aware of the ideas mentioned in the section on focusing on strengths in chapter 7.
5. Support the school. As parents work with their children, they sometimes become frustrated and end up criticizing the school or the teachers. The damaging effects of this upon the child's attitude toward school can be tremendous. If parents have concerns about assignments made or other school matters, they should be encouraged to go to the school and talk it out.
6. Some parents do the work for their children. Sensing increasing frustration, they believe it is easier to do the work than it is to help their children do it. Parents need to be reminded that the objective is to help their children do their schoolwork independently. When frustration is too great, it is time to quit for a while and come back to it another time.

Tutoring More Than One Student.   Tutors will often find that more than one student needs help from them. Teaching two or more students at once is not an uncommon assignment. For example, three students might need to have their spelling reinforced. In such situations group work is more efficient and more fun for the students. Tutors will need some suggestions for working with groups. These suggestions might include the following:

1. Help each student to work to capacity. Do not compare one student with another. Public comparison is, of course, humiliating.
2. If the session starts to drag on and on, change the activity.
3. Try to determine which students work best together. It is often very effective to learn in pairs because students can share their strengths, creating a better final product.
4. Even though students have the same difficulty in school, tutors will need to prepare differentiated assignments to allow for different learning paces and styles.
5. If management difficulties arise, tutors should be encouraged to consult with the coordinator.

Team Tutoring. Occasionally a teaming of tutors will be desirable. Teaming is a complicated procedure, and special training will be needed if it is to be successful. Teaming may be indicated for a number of reasons, some of which are:

1. A beginning tutor can work with an experienced one to assure a good start.
2. A tutor leaving the program can work with the replacement to provide a smooth transition for the students.
3. Two tutors want to work together.
4. Two tutors have a good mix of skills. One might be especially good at motivating students, while the other might be good at planning lessons.
5. Students still receive help even when one tutor is absent. If a tutor is ill or needs to be out of town, the other tutor can continue the program.

The following training ideas are for tutors who are to be teamed:

1. Help tutors to set aside planning time. Teaming takes coordination so that each knows what the other plans to do.
2. Help tutors determine their strengths so that they can use them during instruction.
3. Help tutors plan for evaluation of each session. In this way inefficient practices can be curtailed.
4. Help tutors understand their work load. When one tutor realizes that all of the hard jobs fall upon him or her, then dissatisfaction is quick to set in.

As tutor-training sessions are planned, the coordinator will want to anticipate special problems including those mentioned in this section. Training for special problems can, of course, make tutoring go smoothly and successfully.

FINANCIAL CONSIDERATIONS

All tutoring programs have some costs. Tutors should know how those costs are assumed, and by whom. Schools will normally fulfill reasonable requests for instructional materials. The ability or willingness of schools to pick up other expenses will vary.

Aside from materials for instruction, tutors might need funds for travel, field trips, snacks, and lunches, and they might need to use the school telephone and duplicating facilities and the help of the secretary. All schools have policies regarding funding, and it is the tutor coordinator's responsibility to make those policies known to tutors.

Tutors should also know which people in the school authorize expenditures, and they need to know the procedures to be followed when they request funds.

LEGAL CONSIDERATIONS

Tutors should have in writing the school rules and regulations. As they become members of the school team, they must know and abide by the established rules. Such rules may involve use of school records, expected student behavior, and the location of smoking and eating areas.

Tutors also need to know their liability for the welfare of their students. When the children are in the classroom with the teacher, the teacher is usually responsible. However, when tutoring takes place outside the classroom, the tutor is usually responsible. If tutors are to be responsible, then they should obtain liability insurance.

Student records are ordinarily regarded as private and are not normally available to tutors. When the records are needed, parental permission should be obtained. Even then, tutors will need to know how and when they might enter student records.

Tutors also should know the school regulations regarding testing of students. Some schools require parental permission to give a test that is not a part of the school's normal program. Then tutors will need to know school policy regarding the interpretation and use of test results. In most cases the tutor coordinator or the classroom teacher should be responsible for any test interpretation needed by a tutor.

The school must establish policies regarding tutor responsibility for monitoring student behavior. If student conduct is consistently in violation of school rules, then what is the tutor to do? Once again, the classroom teacher, the tutor coordinator, or the school principal will normally make decisions about poor student behavior.

In case of emergencies, tutors should be prepared to act quickly and effectively. Such events as fires, accidents, and equipment failure can be harmful to students, and quick, appropriate action will be required. Plans for emergency action need to be worked out and understood by each tutor. When there is doubt, the school district's attorney should be consulted to assure appropriate action has been recommended.

TUTORING CHECKLIST

Once you have considered the many aspects of a tutoring program, it is time to begin developing a program to meet the individual needs of your school or project. Figure 26 summarizes major activities discussed in this book and can be used as a guide for developing a tutoring program. Add these ideas to lots of enthusiasm, caring, and organization, and your program will be off to a successful beginning.

FIGURE 26   Checklist for Administrators

Developing a Tutoring Program

	Initiated	Completed
Select a coordinator	_____	_____
Gain support of:		
• teachers	_____	_____
• principal	_____	_____
Make initial decisions		
• content of tutoring	_____	_____
• frequency of sessions	_____	_____
• length of sessions	_____	_____
• number of sessions	_____	_____
• teacher involvement	_____	_____
Recruit tutors		
• develop a recruitment strategy	_____	_____
• interview applicants	_____	_____
Select students for tutoring	_____	_____
Prepare students for tutoring	_____	_____
Find places for tutoring	_____	_____
Assign tutors to students	_____	_____
Establish administrative procedures	_____	_____
Plan initial training sessions	_____	_____
Conduct initial training sessions	_____	_____
Plan in-service training for tutors	_____	_____
Conduct in-service training for tutors	_____	_____
Maintain a support system for tutors	_____	_____
Maintain a support system for students	_____	_____
Evaluate program	_____	_____

Appendices

References and Selected Bibliography

Index

APPENDIX A Sample Parent Permission Form for a Cross-Age Tutoring Program

Dear Parents,

We are in the process of developing a cross-age tutoring program that will involve fifth graders helping second graders. The program is part of a larger county project designed to develop reading skills and positive attitudes toward learning. Children will be tutored three times a week for twenty minutes per session. The fifth graders will assist the second graders through playing reading games and reading together.

Experience in other areas of the country demonstrates that such a program benefits both the student tutors and the children they teach. We anticipate similar benefits in our school.

For the fifth graders, tutoring provides an opportunity to assume a position of responsibility and share knowledge. The training that tutors receive will help them communicate information and develop skill in organizing their thoughts for presentation to others. The second grade students will receive additional individualized reading instruction specifically directed to their needs.

At present our program will be small, involving approximately fifteen students. If, however, it is as successful as we anticipate, we will expand it so more students can participate.

As we initiate this program we are particularly interested in any comments or suggestions you may have. Please call me if you have any questions. My telephone number at home is 582-3051.

> Sincerely,
>
> Roberta Garcia
>
> Teacher

I give permission for my child _____ to participate in the tutoring program.

_____   _____
Parent/Guardian   Date

Please return this to school by October 1. Thank you.

APPENDIX B   Sample Board Games

TICK-TACK-TOE

Materials
- Tick-tack-toe board
- Word cards
- X and O markers

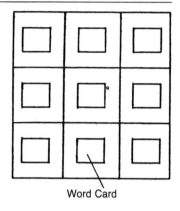

Word Card

Directions
1. Place one word card face down in each square.
2. Players choose either the X or O markers.
3. First player selects word card, reads it, and uses it in a sentence.
4. If player can read word and use it in a sentence accurately, he or she then puts an X or O marker in the square.
5. Players take turns selecting word cards.
6. Player who first gets a straight or diagonal row of X or O is the winner.

DRAG RACE

Materials
- Game board drawn on construction paper
- Trouble Zone cards
- Word cards
- Small cars made of paper to be used as markers
- Die

Directions
1. Put word cards on all spaces of the track.
2. First player rolls die and moves his or her car the number of spaces indicated.
3. If player can read word card on the space and use it in a sentence, he or she stays on the space and follows any directions there may be on that space.

4. If player lands on Trouble Zone, he or she draws a Trouble Zone card and does what it says.
5. Players take turns rolling the die and moving their cars. First player to reach Trophy Square after three laps is the winner.

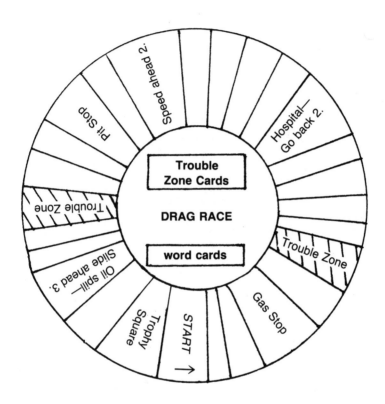

Trouble Zone Cards
1. Flat tire—Go to Pit Stop.
2. Crash—Go to Hospital.
3. Out of gas—Go to Gas Stop.
4. All clear—Take another turn. (Make one-half of all Trouble Zone cards "all clear" cards.)
5. _____ (Make your own.)

APPENDIX C   Tips for Playing Vocabulary Games with Students

1. When your student's answer is correct—
   PRAISE HIM OR HER.
   Say such things as:
   - That's good!
   - Great! You know a lot of words that begin with _____ (beginning letter of correct word).
   - I liked your description of the dog.
2. If your student hesitates when answering—
   a. Give him or her time to think.
   b. After waiting, give a hint such as:
      - The word has the same beginning sound as _____.
      - The word rhymes with _____.
      - A word that means almost the same thing is _____.
3. If your student gives an incorrect answer—
   GIVE THE STUDENT SUPPORT.
   a. Praise him or her for any parts of the answer that may be correct. Then
   b. Say the correct answer. Then
   c. Let him or her repeat the correct answer (when appropriate).
4. When *you* are winning most of the games—
   FIND WAYS FOR YOUR STUDENT TO DO MOST OF THE WINNING.
   You can help your student win more often by taking a turn only when:
   a. a roll of the die shows a two, four, or six;
   b. your student has taken two turns; or
   c. you can spell a word your student has asked you.

APPENDIX D   Tips for Sharing Library Books

TIPS FOR USING BOOKS WITH STUDENTS

T ake at least three library books that you have read to the tutoring session. Consider the students' interests and attention spans in your selection. Let each student choose the book to be read. Be sure to select books you will enjoy too! Your students will be able to tell if you like the stories.

I ntroduce the book in a meaningful way such as:
- telling something interesting you read in the story.
  Example. The story is about Peter who does not have anything to do. One day he gets a big ball of string and he does something that gets him into big trouble.
- asking a question about the title or a picture.
  Example. The lion's name is King. Do you think that might be a good name for him? Let's read the story to find out.

P rovide a comfortable situation for reading. Sit near the students so they can see the illustrations and enjoy the story together.
- Use your voice to heighten interest as you read.
- Involve the students during the story reading when appropriate.

S elect ways to encourage discussion about the story after reading the book.
- Play a questioning game.
  Example. Take turns asking each other questions about things that happened in the book. First ask the student a question like, "Where did Max go in the story?" Then have the student think of a question to ask you. Ask each other two or three questions.
- Talk about a favorite incident or character in the story.

APPENDIX E   Interview Guides

INTERVIEW GUIDE FOR ADULT VOLUNTEER TUTORS

See figure 6 on page 23.

INTERVIEW GUIDE FOR STUDENT VOLUNTEER TUTORS

Name _____ Grade _____

Teacher _____ Room number _____

Brothers or sisters in school   Their teacher's name

_____   _____

_____   _____

Area(s) in which there is a desire to tutor _____

_____

Areas in which tutor would NOT want to instruct _____

_____

Tutor interests and hobbies _____

_____

Travel experiences _____

_____

Activities outside of school _____

_____

Commitment to tutoring _____

_____

APPENDIX F   Starter Ideas for Tutors

1. Use pictures to develop language; to discuss likenesses and differences; to note detail; to classify; to work on opposites, and so forth.
2. Write stories, letters, recipes, and other material with the students.
3. Do science experiments.
4. Use directions for simple craft projects. Example: puppets, weaving.
5. Read stories to students from books, magazines, and newspapers.
6. Play rhyming games.
7. Use flash cards for vocabulary study, math facts, and other drills.
8. Play games to teach left-right. Example: Simon Says.
9. Practice handwriting.
10. Play games to improve auditory and visual memory. Example: "I'm going on a trip."
11. Listen to the students read (a tape recorder can be used for variety).
12. Work with the students' special interests. Example: block-building, puppet-making.
13. Play spelling games.
14. Play active games to develop motor coordination.
15. Fill out applications such as those for social security or library cards.
16. Help the classroom teacher with the follow-up activities.

APPENDIX G A Plan for Inviting Students to Be Tutors in a Reading-Tutoring Program

Meet with groups of students and discuss the following information:

1. *Goals of the Tutoring Program*
   Refer to the special program starting that will involve older students teaching younger ones. The tutors will be helping their students
   - feel good about themselves
   - enjoy their schoolwork
   - increase their skill in reading

2. *Overview of the Tutoring Program*
   Explain the tutoring program including the following points:
   a. Tutors will work with students three times a week for twenty minutes a session during school.
   b. The tutoring sessions will involve playing reading games and reading books.
   c. Tutors will meet at the beginning of the program to get ideas for tutoring and then weekly to share ideas and talk about their teaching.

3. *Type of Student the Tutoring Program Needs*
   Discuss with students that the program needs tutors who would like to work with a younger child, plan activities for him or her, and, most importantly, assume responsibility and work independently. Give examples of types of responsibility, such as going to pick up students or working independently with them. Discuss the activities of the tutoring club to which tutors will belong.

4. *Selection of Student Tutors*
   Tell students that all those who wish to be in the program can submit their names. Since only a few students can be tutors, all names of interested students will be put in a hat. Those whose names are drawn will be the student tutors. If the program is successful and is continued next year, other students will get a chance.

5. *Obtaining Volunteers*
   Ask students if they have any questions about the program. Tell them that a sheet will be sent around the room and that interested students should sign their names. Tell students that the tutors will be selected within the next week and will be notified by their teachers.

APPENDIX H Training Tutors for a
Cross-Age Program in Reading

FIRST TRAINING SESSION

Approximate time: fifty minutes

1. *Introductions*
   Have fifth grade students introduce themselves to the group and put on name tags.
2. *Reasons for the Tutoring Program*
   Ask fifth graders why they want to be in a program that involves working with second graders. Summarize why program was developed, including:
   • helping second graders feel positively about themselves
   • helping second graders enjoy their schoolwork
   • helping second graders increase their skill in reading
   (Use a transparency that includes the above points.)
3. *Overview of the Tutoring Program*
   Explain the program including the following points:
   a. There will be three training sessions to prepare the student tutors. These sessions will include ideas for working with students.
   b. They will work with a second grade buddy three times a week:
      • picking him or her up from class
      • playing a reading game
      • reading with the buddy or helping him or her do assigned classwork
      • taking the buddy back to class after twenty minutes of working together
   c. They will attend weekly meetings with other student tutors to talk about teaching experiences—ideas, problems, and successes.
   (Use a transparency that includes the above points.)
4. *Responsibilities of Student Tutor Position*
   Discuss with the students the honor and responsibility that are associated with the student tutor position. Give them the student tutor agreement (see figure 10) and read it together. Tell students that teachers sign agreements as do people in other professions. Explain that when the training program is finished, the contract

will be signed by the student if he or she wants to be a tutor and by other staff members if they think the student can assume the responsibility.

Have students suggest things that they can do to show they can be responsible when tutoring begins (leaving class quietly at the appropriate time, planning activities for buddies, walking in the halls, being polite and courteous when picking up and working with buddies, cleaning up after working, getting back to class on time).

5. *Use of Student Tutor Folder*
   Give students folders and explain their use:
   - keeping information about tutoring
   - keeping buddies' papers
   Have students put their names on their folders.

6. *Assignment of Second Grade Students*
   Give tutors the lists of tutoring pairs. Have them circle their names and the names of their buddies. Have them also circle the name of the second grade teacher and time and place of tutoring.

7. *Getting to Know Second Grade Buddy*
   Ask students how they think the second grade buddy is going to feel when they first meet (possibly scared, embarrassed). Discuss the kinds of questions they could ask or things they could say to help their buddies feel at ease. Solicit suggestions from students. Role play the situation where a tutor meets a buddy for the first time. Have pairs of students work together to write two questions they could ask their buddies or two statements they could make to help a buddy feel at ease.

   Have students share their ideas with the group. Write ideas on a transparency and tell students the questions will be typed for them each to have.

8. *Helping Buddy Get to Know Student Tutor*
   Ask students if they think their buddies would be interested in knowing about them.

   Discuss ways students can share information about themselves, such as:
   - mentioning things they have in common with buddies
   - talking about similar interests
   - bringing something to show buddies
   Ask students if they can think of something they could bring to share with their buddies.
   Summarize discussion of getting acquainted by showing how these techniques can be used to start each tutoring session.

9. *Preview of Second Session*
    Tell students that the next session will involve making games that
    will help their buddies in the area of reading.

Materials Needed for First Training Session

Name tags	Folders for each student
Student agreement forms	Blank transparency
Lists of tutoring pairs	Overhead projector
Paper and pencils	

SECOND TRAINING SESSION

Approximate time: fifty minutes

1. *Review of First Training Session*
    Review with the students the following topics that were previously
    discussed:
    • tutoring three times a week
    • assignment of tutors
    • ways to get to know buddy
    Give students typed information developed from the last session's
    "Getting to Know Students" questionnaire. Review with students
    that the information they receive from the second graders will give
    them clues as to how to help them feel at ease. Discuss that each
    tutoring session will begin with making their buddies comfortable.

2. *Introduction to Word Games*
    Tell students that after they have helped their buddies feel at ease,
    they will play a game to help them with reading skills.
    Explain procedures:
    a. Each classroom teacher will give tutors words for their buddies
        to learn to read as well as understand.
        Give students the word list from their buddies' teachers. Give
        students examples of how to find out if their buddies know the
        meaning of a word by:
        • showing a word to the tutors
        • asking tutors what the word is
        • asking tutors how they can show that they know the meaning
          of the word (putting it in a sentence, giving a synonym or
          antonym)

b. The words will be used in word games. Refer to one of the purposes of tutoring: to help children enjoy school. Tell tutors that their aim is to try to find the most enjoyable way for their buddies to learn the words.

3. *Making Word Games*

Tell students they are going to have an opportunity to make a game they can use with their buddies. Explain that other game suggestions will also be provided, but that they may know games that are even better and will be able to use them.

Have students divide into two groups to make two different games (groups 1 and 2), or the whole group can make one of the following games:

a. *Group 1. Making and Playing Tick-tack-toe*

Ask group if they have played tick-tack-toe and then review the rules (show playing board—see Appendix B).

Give students packets with blank word cards inside. Ask how they could use words from their word lists and put them into a game like tick-tack-toe. Solicit ideas from students and indicate they can use the word cards.

One procedure:

(1) Place word cards face down on the board.

(2) Players get a turn if they can read the word in the space they want and indicate its meaning.

(3) Players take a turn by either marking board or putting an X or O card in the space.

(4) Winner is the person who can get a straight or diagonal row of X or O.

Have children make a game board, X and O cards, and word cards.

b. *Group 2. Making and Playing Race to the Moon*

Draw as a sample for the tutors a moon and two ladders with six rungs on a piece of construction paper. Place a small piece of paper at the base of each ladder (rocket).

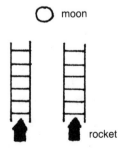

Show students the die and say the aim of the game is to get the rocket to the moon. Give students packets of blank word cards and ask them how they could include the words from their buddies' lists in a game like this. Solicit suggestions.

One procedure:

(1) Each player has a ladder. Players put a word card on each rung of their own ladder. The other word cards are placed face down in a stack between players.

(2) Taking turns, players get to roll the die to move their rockets only if they can read the top word in the stack. After rolling the die and moving the appropriate number, they can stay on the ladder only if they can read the word on the rung. (To make the game harder for tutors, they can only take a turn if the number two, four, or six is rolled.)

(3) Players move their rockets back and forth on the ladder until they have removed all their word cards. When all their cards are off the ladder, they can roll the die to get to the moon.

(4) Winner is first player to get to the moon.

Have the tutors make a game board and word cards for the game.

4. *Homework Assignment*

Tell students to play the game at home and be ready to teach it to another tutor at the next session. Ask them to write each word on their buddy's list twice so there will be two word cards for each word. Give them a handwriting guide to help them remember what the correct printing format looks like. Suggest that the guide might be helpful when printing their cards.

Materials Needed for Second Training Session

Typed questionnaires	Tick-tack-toe board
Individual word lists from teachers	Race to the moon board
Packets with word cards	Dice
Construction paper	Handwriting guides
Pencils and magic markers	

THIRD TRAINING SESSION

Approximate time: fifty minutes

1. *Review Previously Discussed Training Procedures*

Discuss briefly with students the following tutoring procedures:

    a. helping the child feel at ease

    b. playing a reading game with word cards

2. *Tips for Playing Vocabulary Games with Students*

Tell students that they will have an opportunity to play the games they made at the last session.

    Give students "Tips for Playing Reading Games with Students" (see Appendix C). Discuss each item on the sheet. Ask the following types of questions for each item:

    a. After discussing No. 1, ask students what they could say if a child said *house* correctly. Solicit suggestions (such as, "You know a lot of words that begin like *hot*").

    b. After discussing No. 2, ask students what kind of hint they could give for a word like *hit*.

    c. After discussing No. 3, ask students what they could do if a child said *pop* for *hop* (say the word correctly and let student repeat it).

    d. After discussing No. 4, ask what other ways they know of to help the student win.

3. *Practice Playing Reading Game*

Have students role play the tutoring situation, one being the student and the other the tutor. Pair students who were working in different groups during the second session. Have students refer to their guidelines for playing reading games. Give students list of game ideas to use as reference for other session.

4. *Guidelines for Reading Books to Students*

Explain last step of tutoring procedure, which is tutors reading books *to* students or *with* students. Give students lists that will help them select books. Explain TIPS (see Appendix D). Explain difference between reading books *with* and *to* students.

    a. Books to read *with* students are books that a second grader might be able to read.

    b. Books to read *to* students are a little more difficult, and second-grade students might have difficulty reading them by themselves.

    Let students pick a few books they would be interested in reading. Suggest students see the librarian or media center director if they need help finding more books.

5. *Use of Student Logs*

Give students their logs (see figure 13).

    Discuss the logs including the following sections:

    a. Plans—This section is to be used before working with a buddy. This is where you write what game you are going to play and the book you are going to read or books you are going to bring to the tutoring session. Discuss how important it is to plan so you can bring everything you need for the session. Ask students when they can plan (at home, free time at school). Let them write in plans for first tutoring session.

b. Comments—Here you write what happened and list successes, problems, and ideas for next session. This is important because it provides a record of what went on in previous sessions and gives ideas for other sessions. Explain that it does not have to be very long and is best written as soon after tutoring as possible.

c. Feelings—The lines under the question about how you feel about tutoring are to be filled in with a description of your feelings. You might want to use just a one-word description or a smiling, bland, or frowning face.

d. Check plans completed—After tutoring put a check next to things you did, and then you will know if you did what you planned.

6. *Signing of Student Agreements*

Tell the students that they are now fully approved (if indeed they are) for participation in the tutoring program, and that their agreements can now be signed (see figure 10). Review with them that signing the agreement means they are going to fulfill their responsibilities as stated there. Read the agreement aloud and have students, principal, and program coordinator sign it. Have agreements taken to class for the teachers' signatures. Give one copy to the student and have program coordinator keep the other.

7. *Final Question-and-Answer Session*

Ask group for any questions they may have about tutoring. Set time for next tutor meeting and have students write it down. Assure students that the program coordinator will be available to help if there are any problems during tutoring. Give students times during the day or week when the coordinator is generally free to answer questions and give suggestions.

Materials Needed for Third Training Session

Student logs
Books on second-grade level that tutors can sign out
Student agreements
Overhead projector
Book lists
Game lists

APPENDIX I   Checklist for the First Day of Tutoring

Do you have the following information?	Check the box when you have the information

1. _____ ☐
   Student's name

2. _____ ☐
   Day and time of tutoring

3. _____ ☐
   Place of tutoring

4. _____ ☐
   Place to pick up student

5. Plans for tutoring

   List of get-acquainted questions ☐
   High interest activity ☐
   An extra activity ☐

6. _____   _____
   School contact person   Telephone

7. General school procedures

   Fire emergency_____ ☐

   Health emergency_____ ☐

   Dress code_____ ☐

   Parking_____ ☐

REFERENCES AND SELECTED BIBLIOGRAPHY

REFERENCES

Devin-Sheehan, L.; Feldman, R. S.; and Allen, V. "Research on Children Tutoring Children: A Critical Review." *Review of Educational Research,* 46 (Summer 1976): 355–85.

Koskinen, Patricia S. "An Investigation of the Effects of Cross-Age Tutoring on the Self-Concept and Knowledge and Word Meaning of Fifth-Grade Tutors and Their Second-Grade Tutees." Doctoral dissertation, University of Maryland, 1975.

Lippitt, Peggy. "Children Can Teach Other Children." *The Instructor,* 9 (May 1969): 41.

A SELECTED BIBLIOGRAPHY FOR TEACHERS AND ADMINISTRATORS

Adult Literacy Program Handbook. DHEW Publications No. 017–080–01917–5. Washington, D.C.: U.S. Government Printing Office, 1980.

Allen, A. R., and Boraks, N. "Peer Tutoring: Putting it to the Test." *Reading Teacher,* 32 (December 1978): 274–78.

Allen, V., ed. *Children as Teachers.* New York: Academic Press, 1976.

Bloom, S. *Peer and Cross-Age Tutoring in the Schools.* Washington, D.C.: U.S. Department of Health, Education and Welfare, National Institute of Education, December 1976.

Boraks, N., and Allen, A. R. "A Program to Enhance Peer Tutoring." *The Reading Teacher,* 30 (February 1977): 479–84.

Carter, B., and Dapper, G. *Organizing School Volunteer Programs.* New York: Citation Press, 1974.

————. *School Volunteers: What They Do and How They Do It.* New York: Citation Press, 1971.

Criscuolo, N. P. "Training Tutors Effectively." *The Reading Teacher,* 25 (November 1971): 157–59.

Devin-Sheehan, L.; Feldman, R. S.; and Allen, V. "Research on Children Tutoring Children: A Critical Review." *Review of Educational Research,* 46 (Summer 1976): 355–85.

Ehly, S. W., and Larson, S. C. *Peer Tutoring for Individualized Instruction.* Boston: Allyn & Bacon, 1980.

Gartner, A.; Kohler, M.; and Riessman, F. *Children Teach Children.* New York: Harper & Row, 1971.

Gibbons, B. *Random House HOSTS Help One Student to Succeed.* New York: Random House, 1975.

Gold, P., and Taylor, A. M. "Of Course, Volunteers." *The Reading Teacher,* 28 (April 1975): 614–16.

Howard, K. "A Peer Tutoring Program in a Technical School." *Journal of Reading,* 21 (November 1977): 115–20.

Mavrogenes, N. A., and Galen, N. D. "Cross-Age Tutoring: Why and How." *Journal of Reading,* 22 (January 1979): 344–53.

Melaragno, R. J. "Beyond Decoding: Systematic Schoolwide Tutoring in Reading." *The Reading Teacher,* 28 (November 1974): 157–60.

———— *Tutoring with Students: A Handbook for Establishing Tutorial Programs in School.* Englewood Cliffs, N.J.: Educational Technology Publications, 1976.

Niedermeyer, F. C., and Ellis, P. "Remedial Reading Instruction by Trained Pupil Tutors." *Elementary School Journal,* 71 (April 1971): 400–05.

Pellegrene, T., and Dickerson, F. E. "Student Tutors Are Effective." *Journal of Reading,* 20 (March 1977): 466–68.

Project Voice. *How To Do Handbook for Coordinators of Volunteers in Education.* Washington, D.C.: Washington Technical Institute, U.S. Office of Education, 1971.

Rauch, S. J. *Handbook for the Volunteer Tutor.* Newark, Del.: International Reading Association, 1969.

Robb, M. H. *Teacher Assistants.* Columbus, Ohio: Merrill, 1969.

Smith, C.B. *Volunteer Programs That Work: Getting People to Read.* New York: Delacorte Press, 1973.

Snow, L. *Using Teacher Aides.* Highland Park, N.J.: Drier Educational Systems, 1972.

Tutors' Resource Handbook; Tutor-Trainers' Resource Handbook; Tutoring

Resource Handbook for Teachers. DHEW Publications No. (OE) 74-00101; 74-00102; 74-00103. Washington, D.C.: U.S. Government Printing Office, 1976.

Wolf, A. D. *Tutoring Is Caring: You Can Help Someone to Read.* Altoona, Pa.: Montessori Learning Center, 1976.

Index

An "F" after a page number indicates that the information is contained in a figure.